W9-AUL-273

GREATEST SPORTS MOMENTS

DEFYING HITLER

JESSE OWENS' OLYMPIC TRIUMPH

BY NEL YOMTOV
ILLUSTRATED BY EDUARDO GARCIA AND RED WOLF STUDIO

CONSULTANT:
BRUCE BERGLUND
PROFESSOR OF HISTORY, CALVIN COLLEGE
GRAND RAPIDS, MICHIGAN

X
GN

CAPSTONE PRESS

Graphic Library is published by Capstone Press,
1710 Roe Crest Drive, North Mankato, Minnesota 56003
www.mycapstone.com

Library of Congress Cataloging-in-Publication data
Names: Yomtov, Nelson author. | Garcia, Eduardo, 1970 August 31– illustrator.
Title: Defying Hitler : Jesse Owens' Olympic triumph / by Nel Yomtov ; illustrated by Eduardo Garcia.
Description: North Mankato, Minnesota : Graphic Library, an imprint of Capstone Press, [2018] | Series: Greatest Sports Moments | Includes index. | Audience: Ages: 8–14.
Identifiers: LCCN 2018001970 (print) | LCCN 2018005149 (ebook) | ISBN 9781543528732 (eBook PDF) | ISBN 9781543528657 (hardcover) | ISBN 9781543528695 (paperback)
Subjects: LCSH: Owens, Jesse, 1913–1980—Juvenile literature. | African American track and field athletes—Biography—Juvenile literature. | Olympic Games (11th : 1936 : Berlin, Germany)—Juvenile literature.
Classification: LCC GV697.09 (ebook) | LCC GV697.09 Y65 2018 (print) | DDC 796.42092 [B]—dc23
LC record available at https://lccn.loc.gov/2018001970

Summary: Tells the story of Jesse Owens' achievements at the 1936 Summer Olympics in Berlin, Germany in defiance of Adolf Hitler and his racist views of white supremacy.

EDITOR
Aaron J. Sautter

ART DIRECTOR
Nathan Gassman

DESIGNER
Ted Williams

MEDIA RESEARCHER
Eric Gohl

PRODUCTION SPECIALIST
Laura Manthe

Shutterstock: Pedjami

Direct quotations appear in ***bold italicized text*** on the following pages:

Pages 7 (panels 1 and 2), 18 (panel 2): from *Jesse Owens: Facing Down Hitler* by Jackie F. Stanmyre. New York: Cavendish Square Publishing, 2016.
Pages 8 (panel 2), 10 (panels 1 and 2), 12 (panel 2), 13 (panel 3), 18 (panel 3), 22 (panel 1), 25 (panels 1 and 2), 27 (panel 1): from *Triumph: The Untold Story of Jesse Owens and Hitler's Olympics* by Jeremy Schaap. New York: Houghton Mifflin, 2007.
Page 9 (panels 3 and 4): from *Jesse Owens: Gold Medal Hero* by Jim Gigliotti. New York: Sterling, 2010.
Page 18 (panel 2): from *The Jesse Owens Story* by Jesse Owens. New York: G.P. Putnam's Sons, 1970.
Page 24 (panel 2): from *Jesse Owens: An Americal Life* by William J. Baker. New York: Free Press/div. of Macmillan, 1986.

Printed and bound in the United states of America.
PA017

TABLE OF CONTENTS

A DATE WITH DESTINY 4

CHALLENGING THE NAZIS. 6

RECORD-BREAKING RUNNER. 10

BRINGING HOME THE GOLD 16

THE FINAL RUN 24

MEETING LIFE'S CHALLENGES 28

GLOSSARY. 30

READ MORE 31

CRITICAL THINKING QUESTIONS 31

INTERNET SITES. 32

INDEX 32

A DATE WITH DESTINY

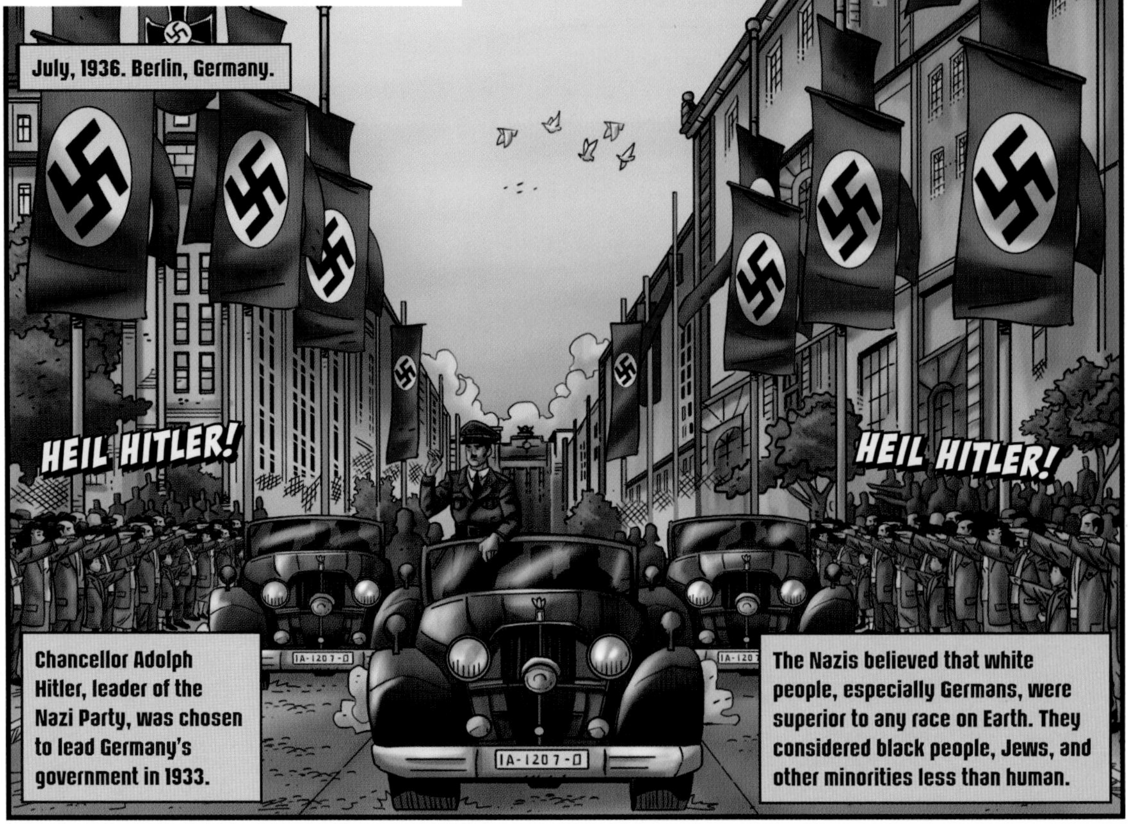
July, 1936. Berlin, Germany.
HEIL HITLER!
HEIL HITLER!
Chancellor Adolph Hitler, leader of the Nazi Party, was chosen to lead Germany's government in 1933.
The Nazis believed that white people, especially Germans, were superior to any race on Earth. They considered black people, Jews, and other minorities less than human.

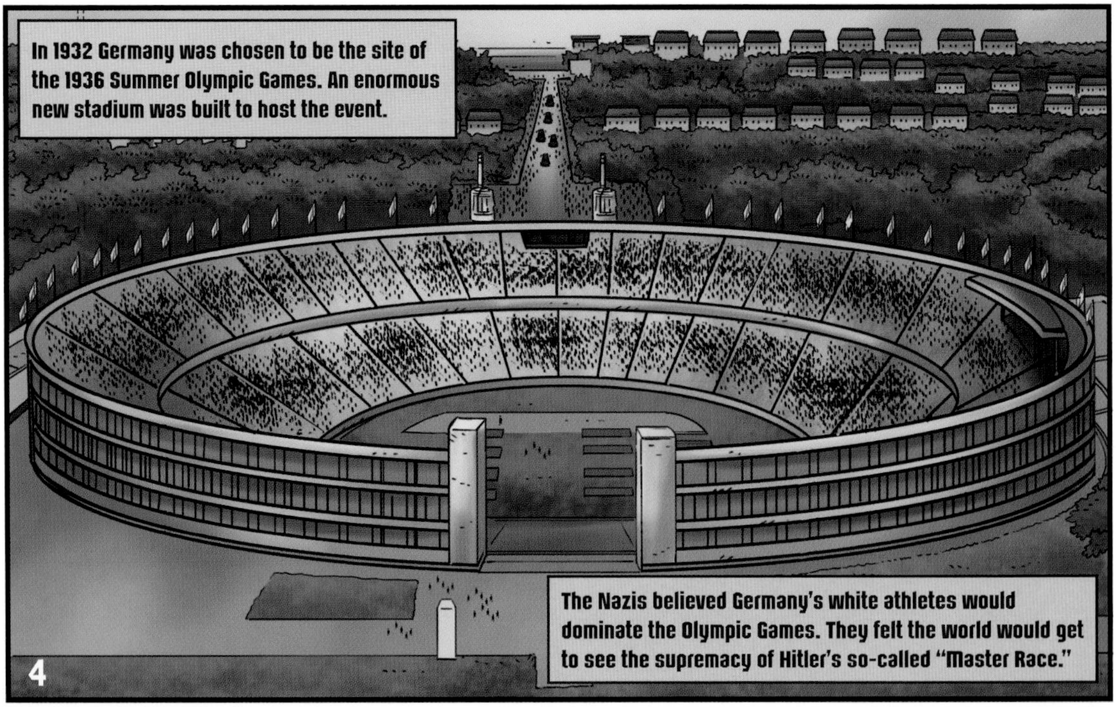
In 1932 Germany was chosen to be the site of the 1936 Summer Olympic Games. An enormous new stadium was built to host the event.
The Nazis believed Germany's white athletes would dominate the Olympic Games. They felt the world would get to see the supremacy of Hitler's so-called "Master Race."

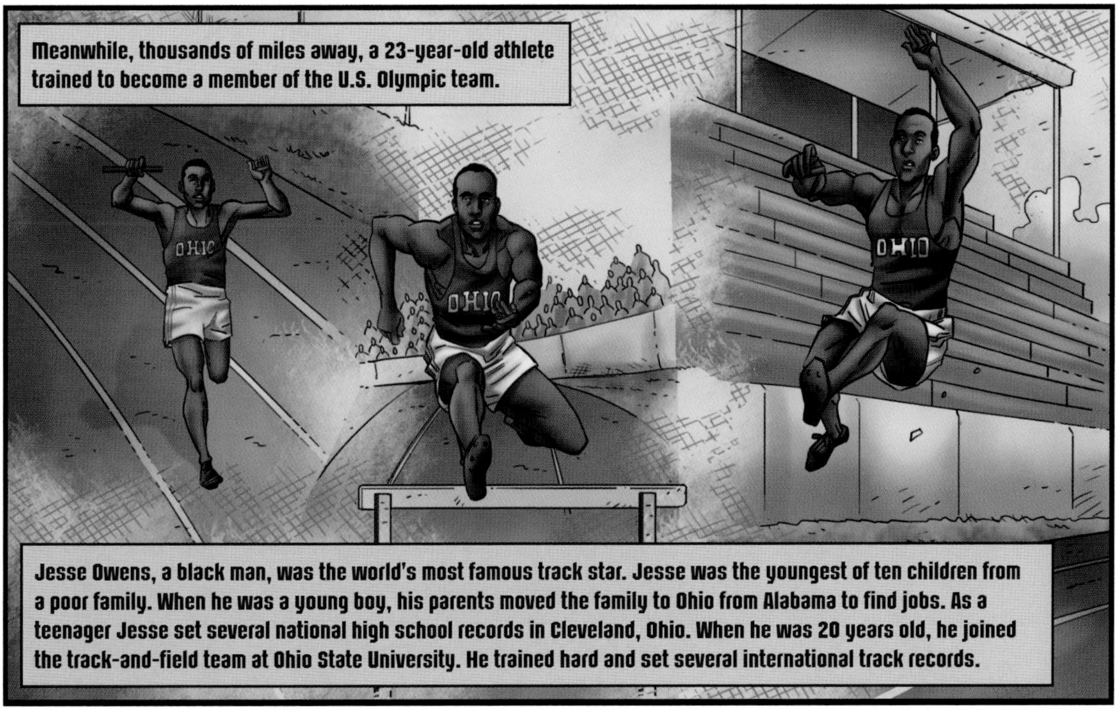
Meanwhile, thousands of miles away, a 23-year-old athlete trained to become a member of the U.S. Olympic team.
OHIO
OHIO
OHIO
Jesse Owens, a black man, was the world's most famous track star. Jesse was the youngest of ten children from a poor family. When he was a young boy, his parents moved the family to Ohio from Alabama to find jobs. As a teenager Jesse set several national high school records in Cleveland, Ohio. When he was 20 years old, he joined the track-and-field team at Ohio State University. He trained hard and set several international track records.

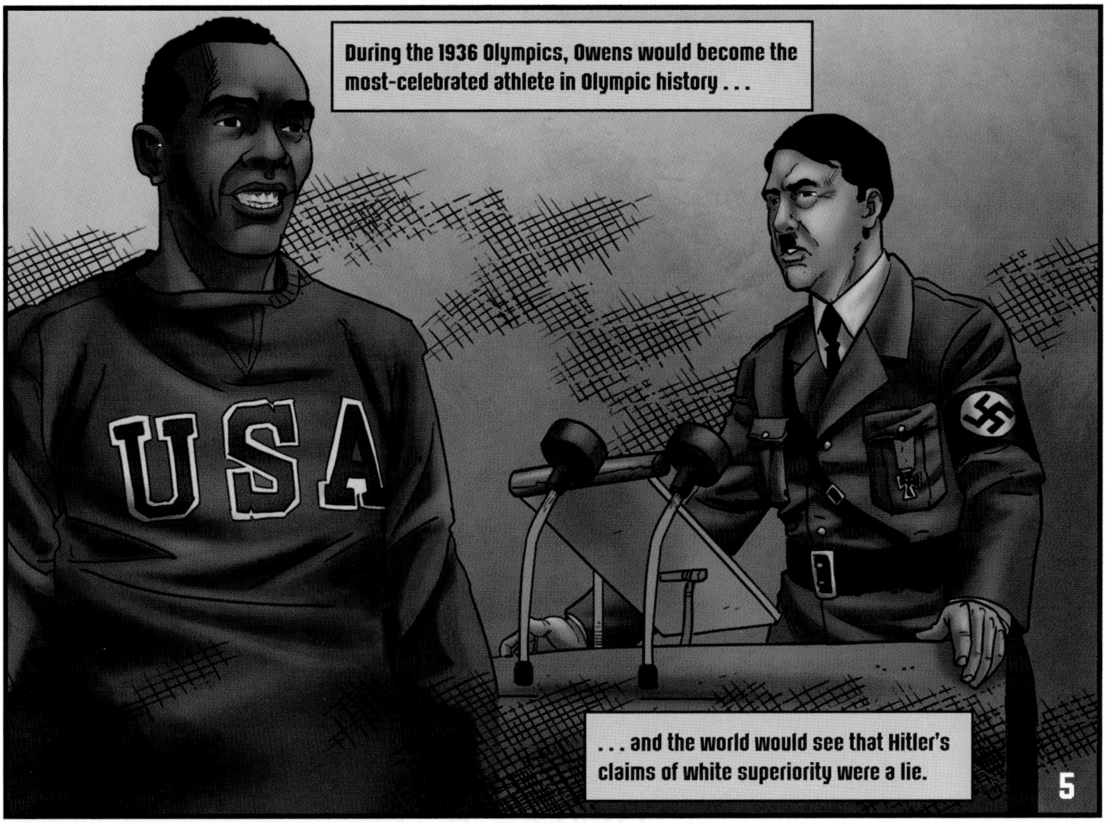
During the 1936 Olympics, Owens would become the most-celebrated athlete in Olympic history . . .
USA
. . . and the world would see that Hitler's claims of white superiority were a lie.

CHALLENGING THE NAZIS

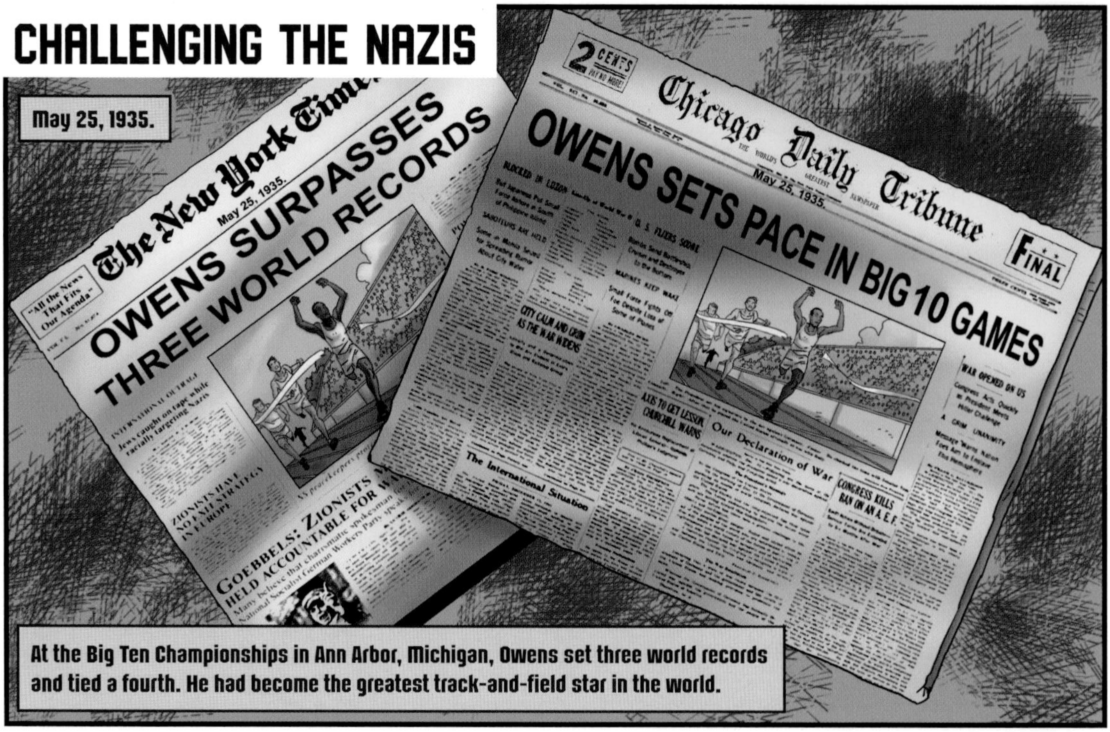
May 25, 1935.
The New York Times
May 25, 1935.
"All the News That Fits Our Agenda"
OWENS SURPASSES THREE WORLD RECORDS
GOEBBELS: ZIONISTS HELD ACCOUNTABLE FOR W
2 CENTS
Chicago Daily Tribune
May 25, 1935.
FINAL
OWENS SETS PACE IN BIG 10 GAMES
Our Declaration of War
The International Situation
At the Big Ten Championships in Ann Arbor, Michigan, Owens set three world records and tied a fourth. He had become the greatest track-and-field star in the world.

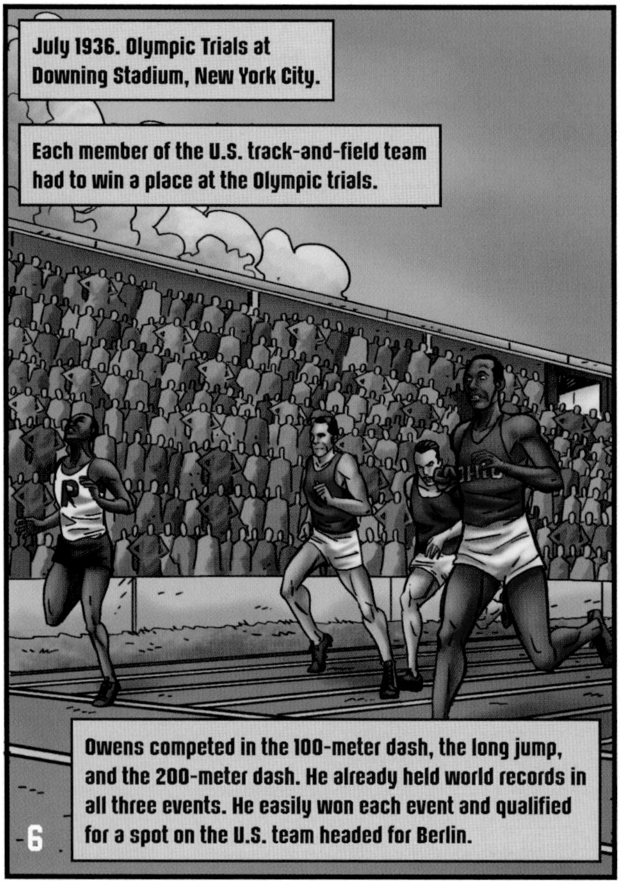
July 1936. Olympic Trials at Downing Stadium, New York City.
Each member of the U.S. track-and-field team had to win a place at the Olympic trials.
Owens competed in the 100-meter dash, the long jump, and the 200-meter dash. He already held world records in all three events. He easily won each event and qualified for a spot on the U.S. team headed for Berlin.

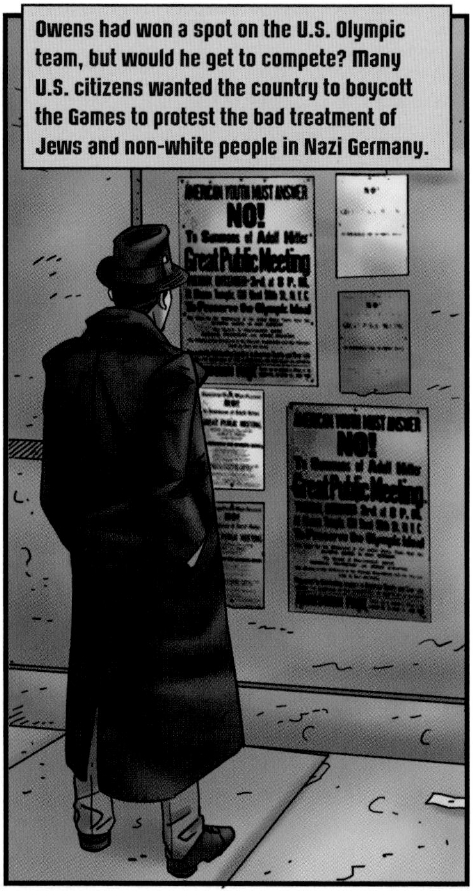
Owens had won a spot on the U.S. Olympic team, but would he get to compete? Many U.S. citizens wanted the country to boycott the Games to protest the bad treatment of Jews and non-white people in Nazi Germany.
AMERICAN YOUTH MUST ANSWER
NO!
Great Public Meeting
AMERICAN YOUTH MUST ANSWER
NO!
Great Public Meeting

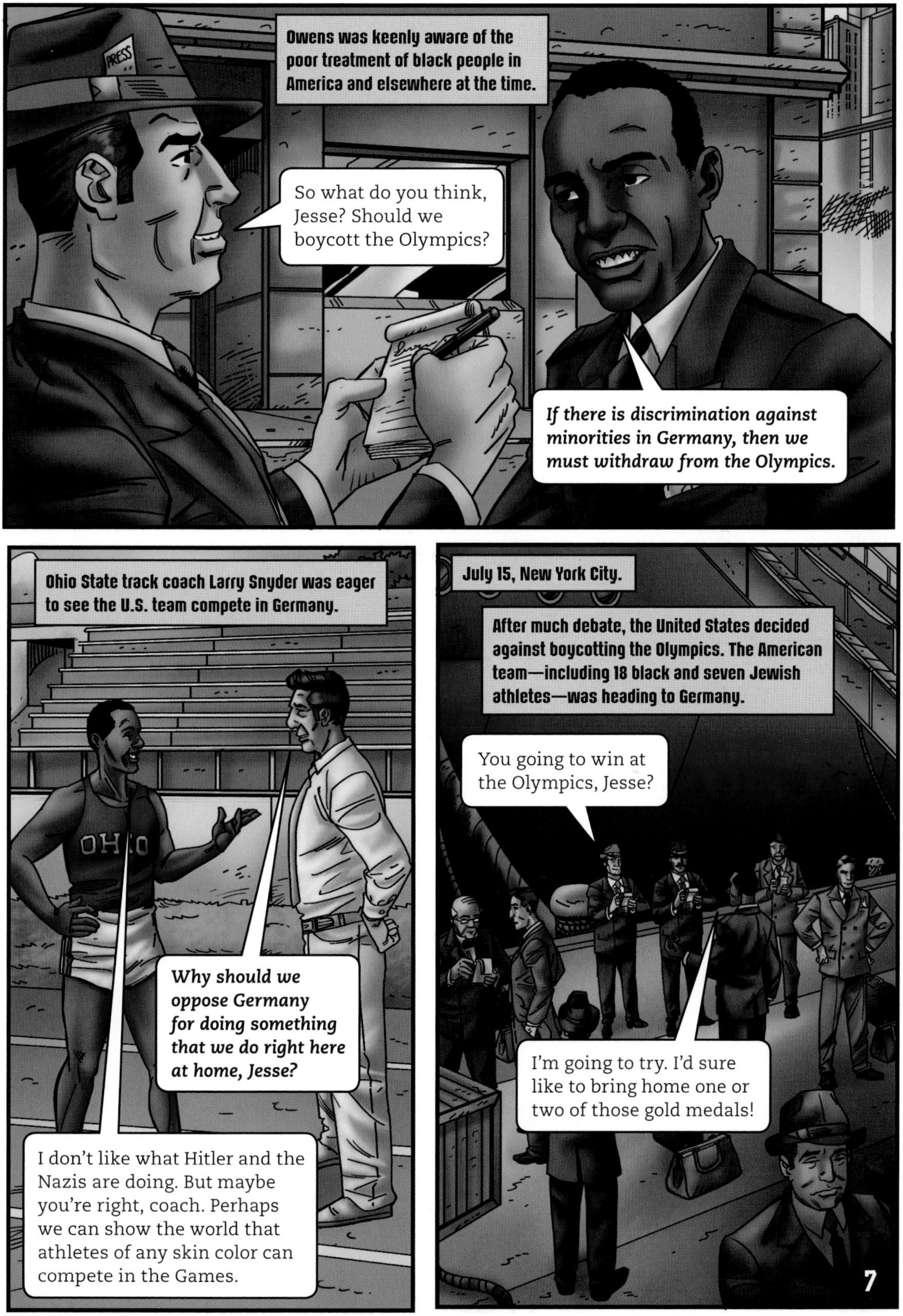
Owens was keenly aware of the poor treatment of black people in America and elsewhere at the time.
PRESS
So what do you think, Jesse? Should we boycott the Olympics?
If there is discrimination against minorities in Germany, then we must withdraw from the Olympics.
Ohio State track coach Larry Snyder was eager to see the U.S. team compete in Germany.
OHIO
Why should we oppose Germany for doing something that we do right here at home, Jesse?
I don't like what Hitler and the Nazis are doing. But maybe you're right, coach. Perhaps we can show the world that athletes of any skin color can compete in the Games.
July 15, New York City.
After much debate, the United States decided against boycotting the Olympics. The American team—including 18 black and seven Jewish athletes—was heading to Germany.
You going to win at the Olympics, Jesse?
I'm going to try. I'd sure like to bring home one or two of those gold medals!

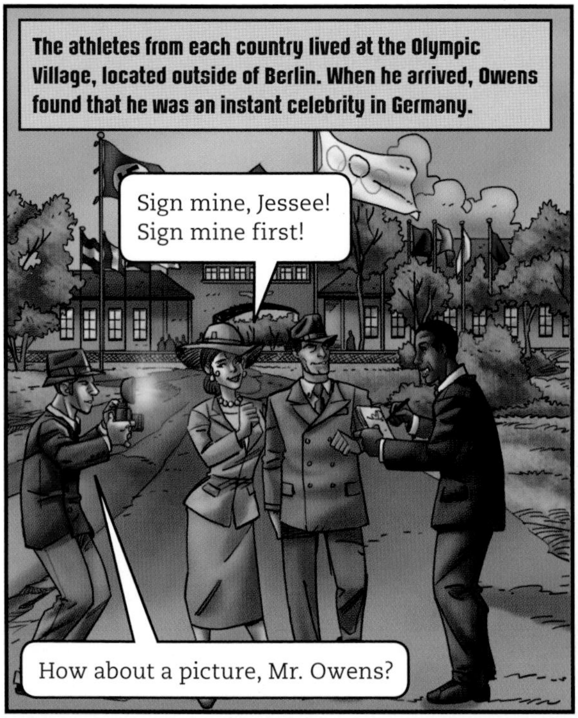
The athletes from each country lived at the Olympic Village, located outside of Berlin. When he arrived, Owens found that he was an instant celebrity in Germany.
Sign mine, Jessee! Sign mine first!
How about a picture, Mr. Owens?

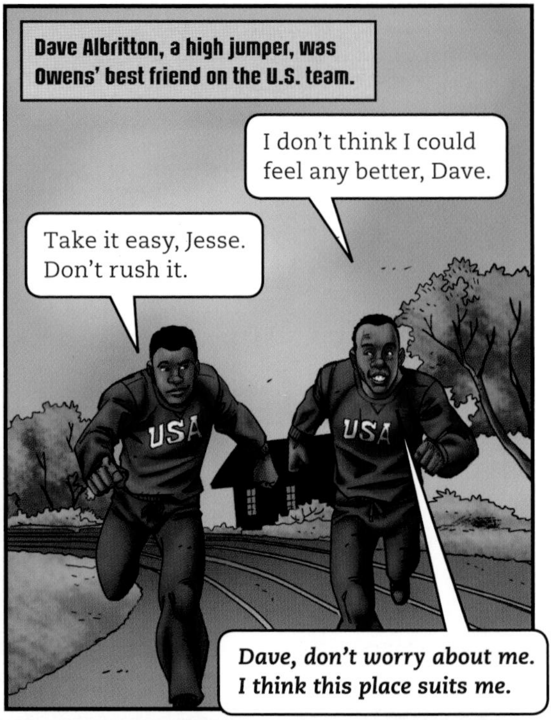
Dave Albritton, a high jumper, was Owens' best friend on the U.S. team.
I don't think I could feel any better, Dave.
Take it easy, Jesse. Don't rush it.
USA
USA
Dave, don't worry about me. I think this place suits me.

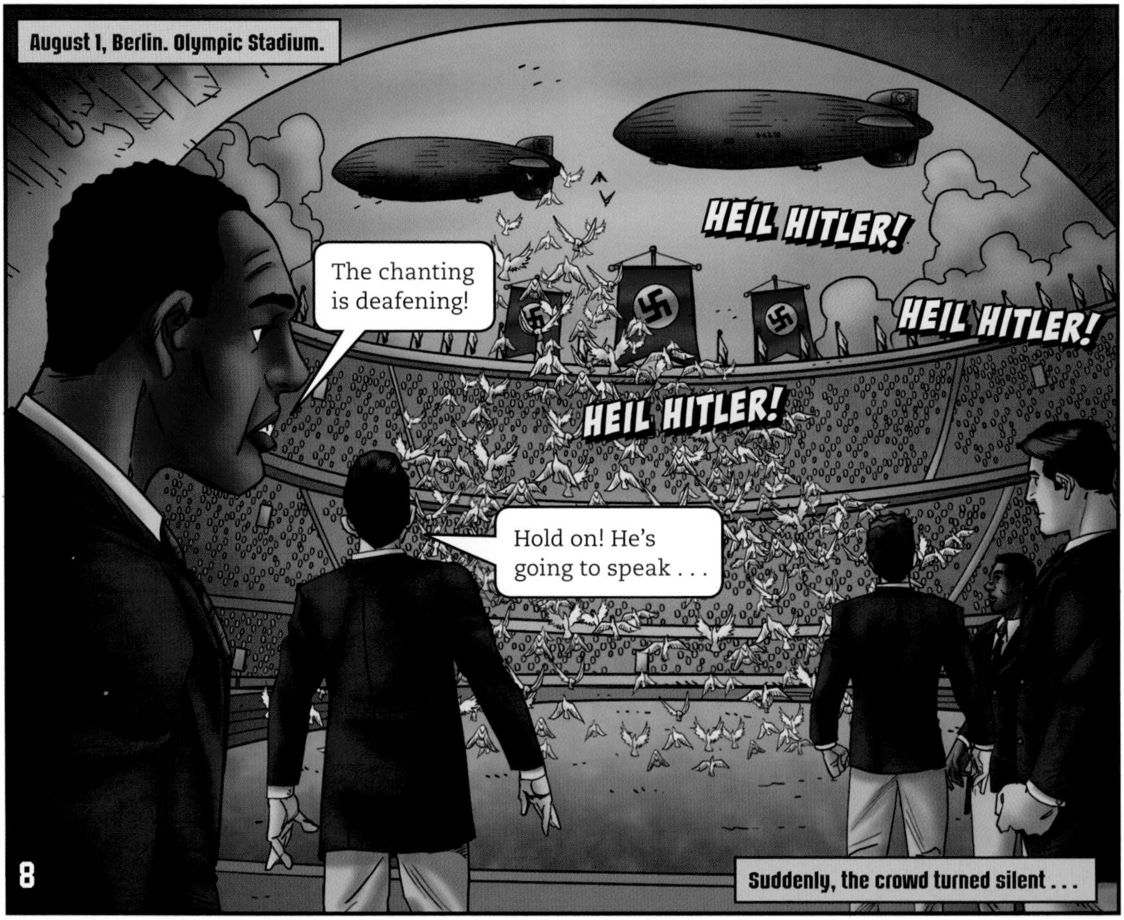
August 1, Berlin. Olympic Stadium.
HEIL HITLER!
HEIL HITLER!
The chanting is deafening!
HEIL HITLER!
Hold on! He's going to speak . . .
Suddenly, the crowd turned silent . . .

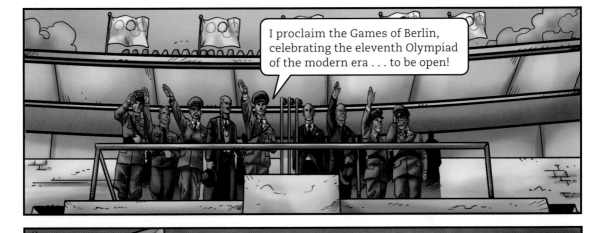

I proclaim the Games of Berlin, celebrating the eleventh Olympiad of the modern era . . . to be open!

Did you see how some countries' teams gave Hitler the Nazi salute with their right arm?

Yeah. And some even dipped their flags to him. I'm glad we're not doing any of that.

The U.S. team refused to salute Hitler or dip the U.S. flag. The German crowd was displeased.

The German people have treated me well, but black people are everything Hitler hates. Hitler hates my skin . . .

But I'm not here to play politics. I'm here to win medals. All these years of hard work—I'm going to make sure they were worthwhile.

RECORD-BREAKING RUNNER

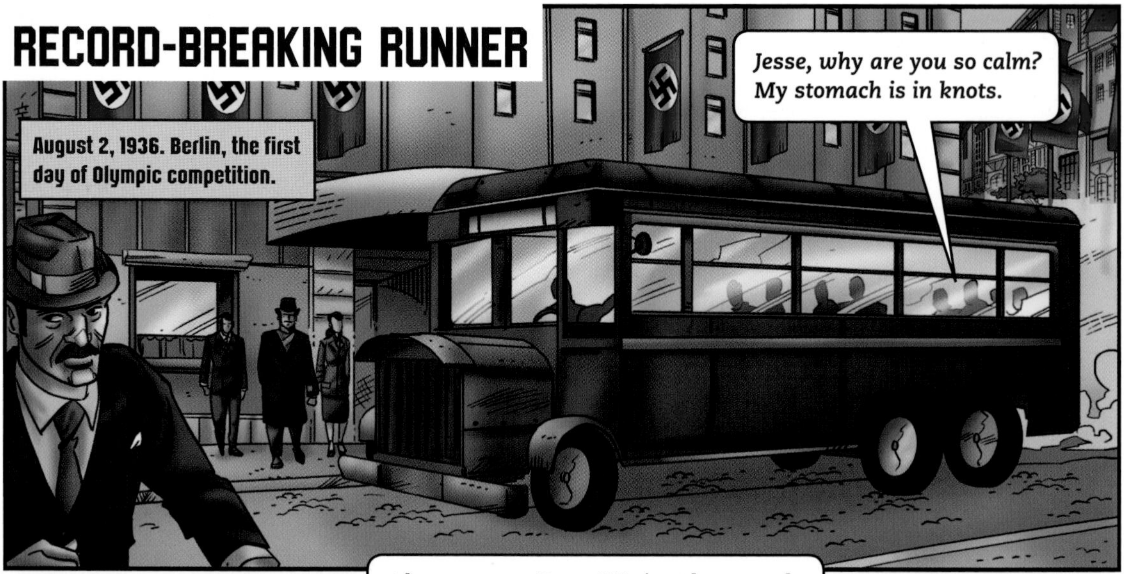
August 2, 1936. Berlin, the first day of Olympic competition.
Jesse, why are you so calm? My stomach is in knots.

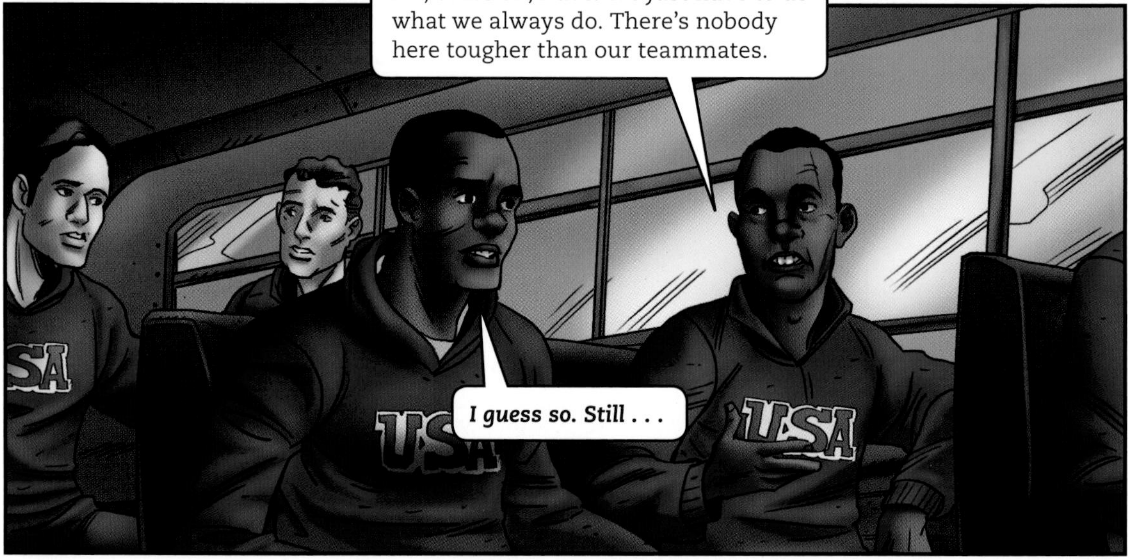
Ah, come on, Dave. We just have to do what we always do. There's nobody here tougher than our teammates.
I guess so. Still . . .

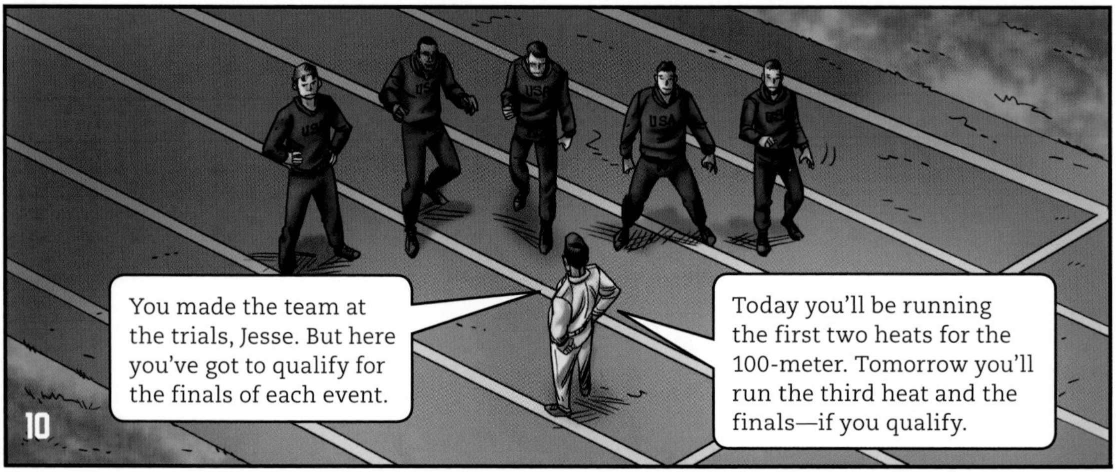
You made the team at the trials, Jesse. But here you've got to qualify for the finals of each event.
Today you'll be running the first two heats for the 100-meter. Tomorrow you'll run the third heat and the finals—if you qualify.

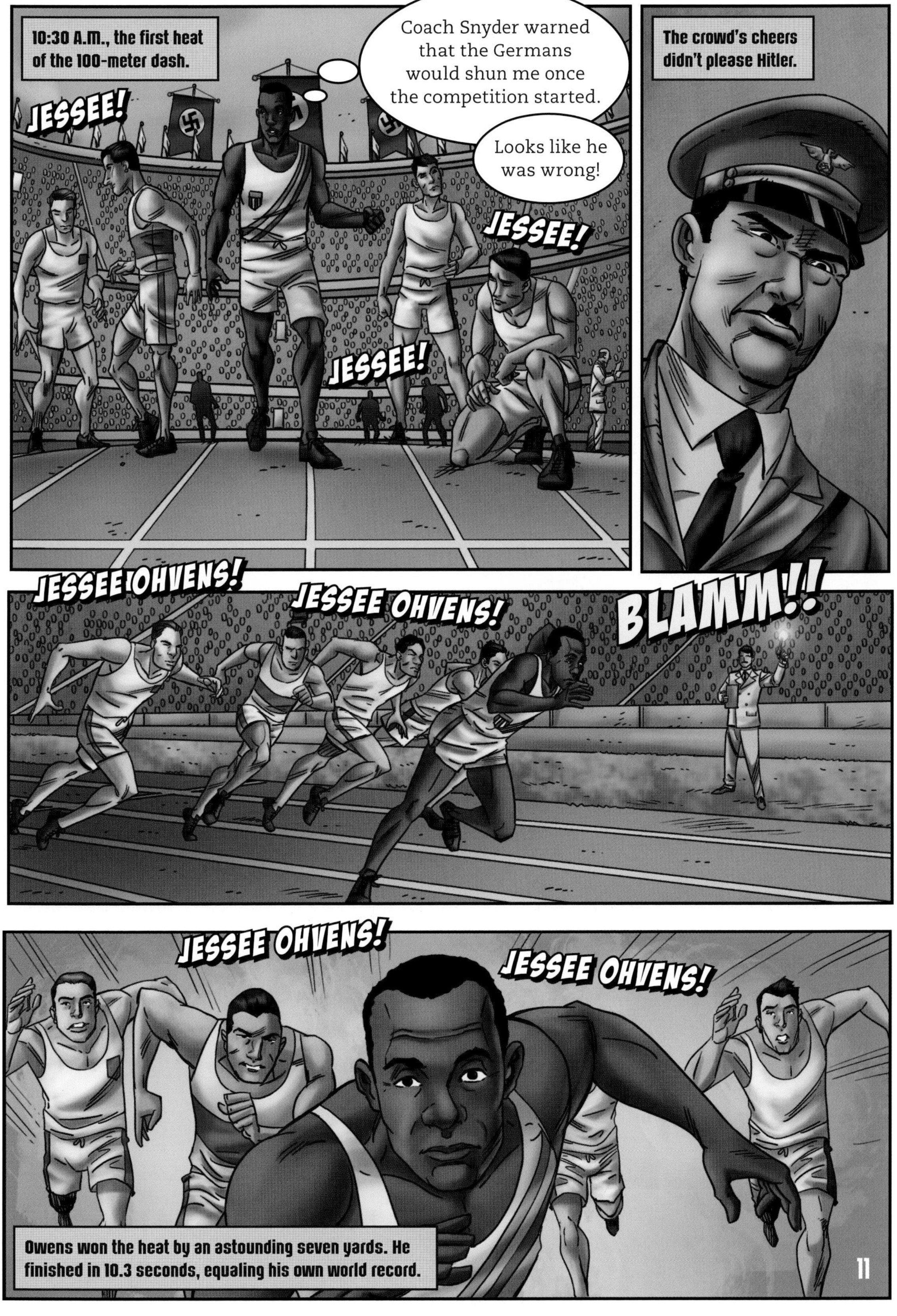
10:30 A.M., the first heat of the 100-meter dash.
Coach Snyder warned that the Germans would shun me once the competition started.
JESSEE!
Looks like he was wrong!
JESSEE!
JESSEE!
The crowd's cheers didn't please Hitler.
JESSEE OHVENS!
JESSEE OHVENS!
BLAMM!!
JESSEE OHVENS!
JESSEE OHVENS!
Owens won the heat by an astounding seven yards. He finished in 10.3 seconds, equaling his own world record.

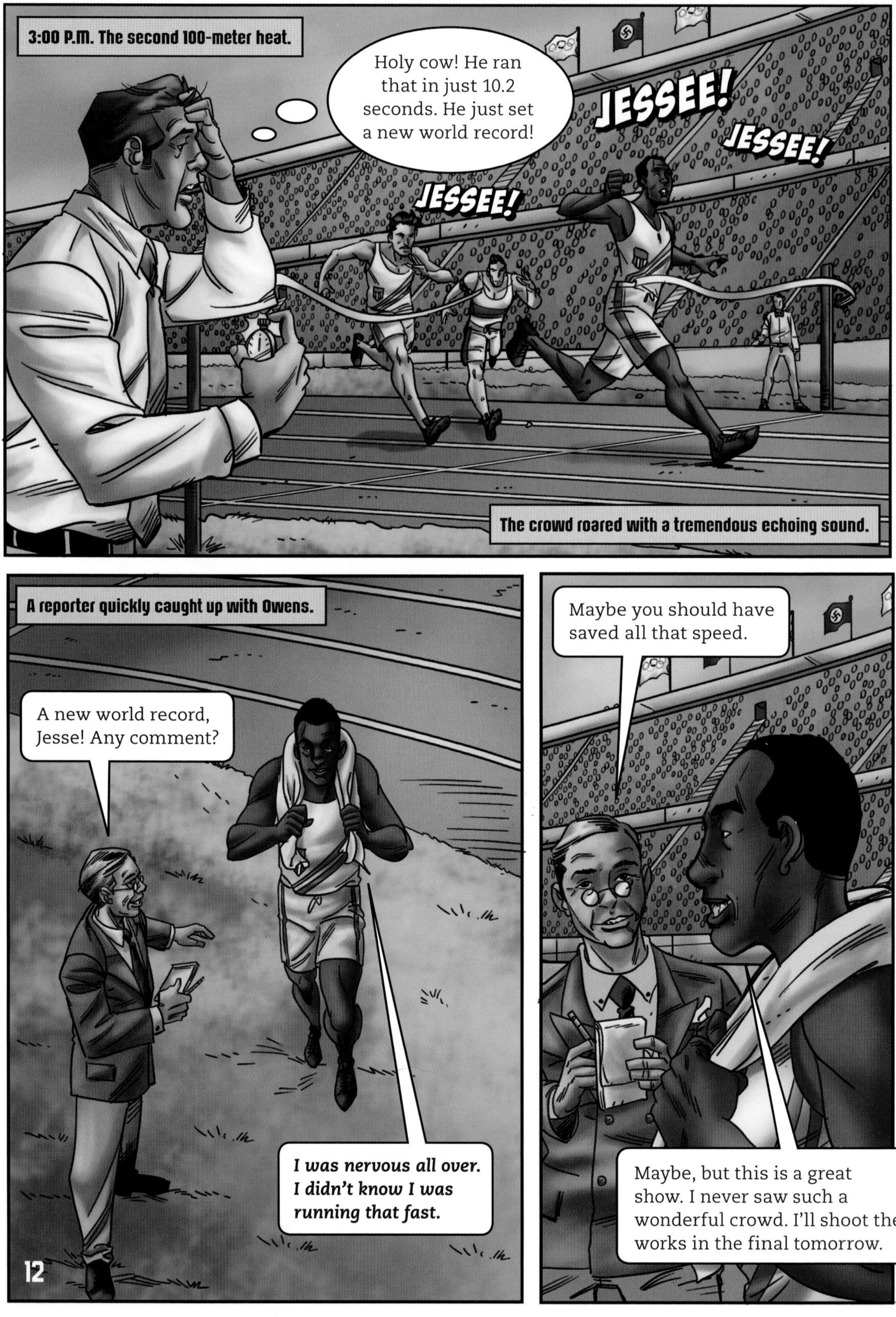
3:00 P.M. The second 100-meter heat.
Holy cow! He ran that in just 10.2 seconds. He just set a new world record!
JESSEE!
JESSEE!
JESSEE!
The crowd roared with a tremendous echoing sound.
A reporter quickly caught up with Owens.
A new world record, Jesse! Any comment?
I was nervous all over. I didn't know I was running that fast.
Maybe you should have saved all that speed.
Maybe, but this is a great show. I never saw such a wonderful crowd. I'll shoot the works in the final tomorrow.

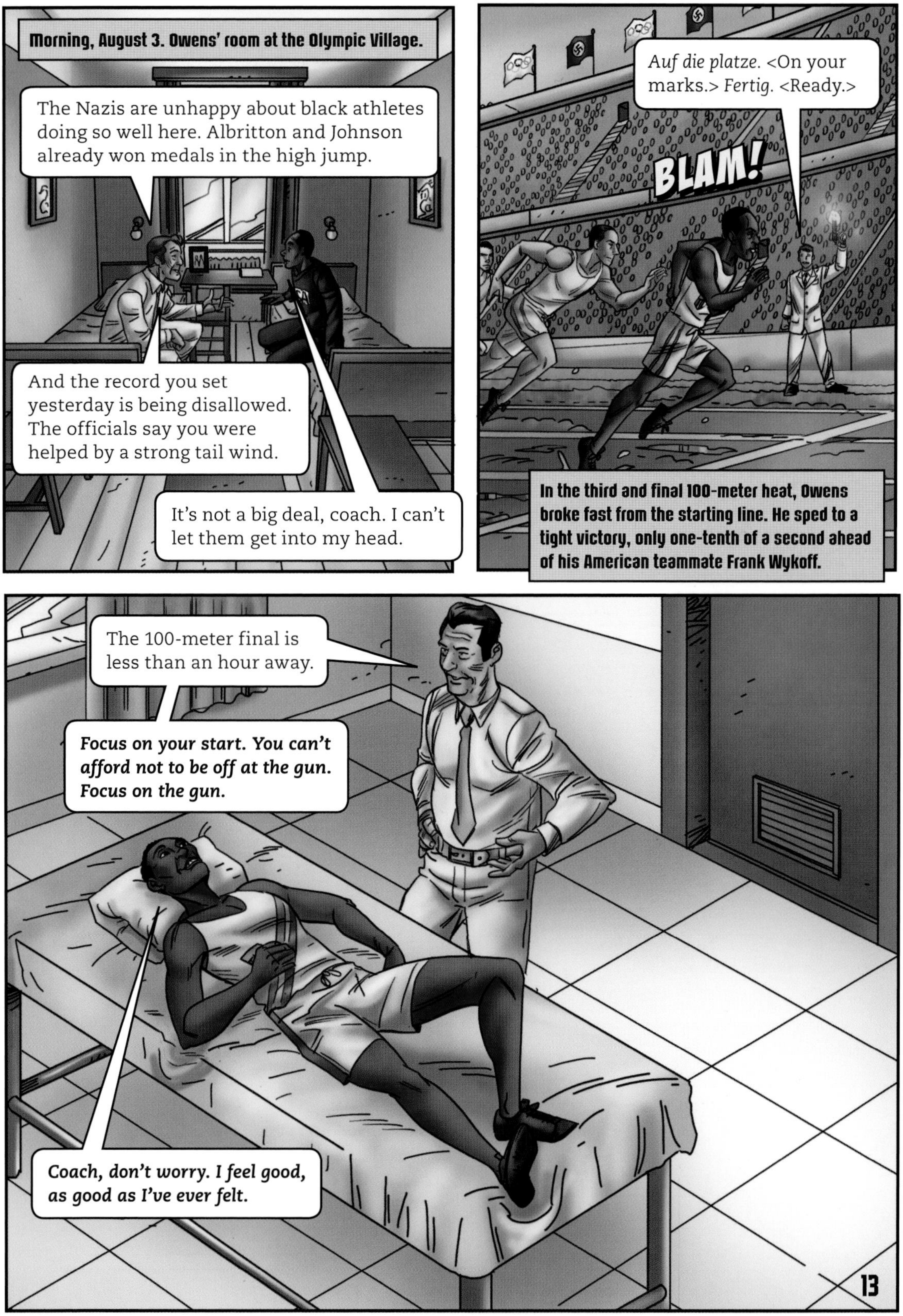
Morning, August 3. Owens' room at the Olympic Village.
The Nazis are unhappy about black athletes doing so well here. Albritton and Johnson already won medals in the high jump.
And the record you set yesterday is being disallowed. The officials say you were helped by a strong tail wind.
It's not a big deal, coach. I can't let them get into my head.
Auf die platze. <On your marks.> *Fertig.* <Ready.>
BLAM!
In the third and final 100-meter heat, Owens broke fast from the starting line. He sped to a tight victory, only one-tenth of a second ahead of his American teammate Frank Wykoff.
The 100-meter final is less than an hour away.
Focus on your start. You can't afford not to be off at the gun. Focus on the gun.
Coach, don't worry. I feel good, as good as I've ever felt.

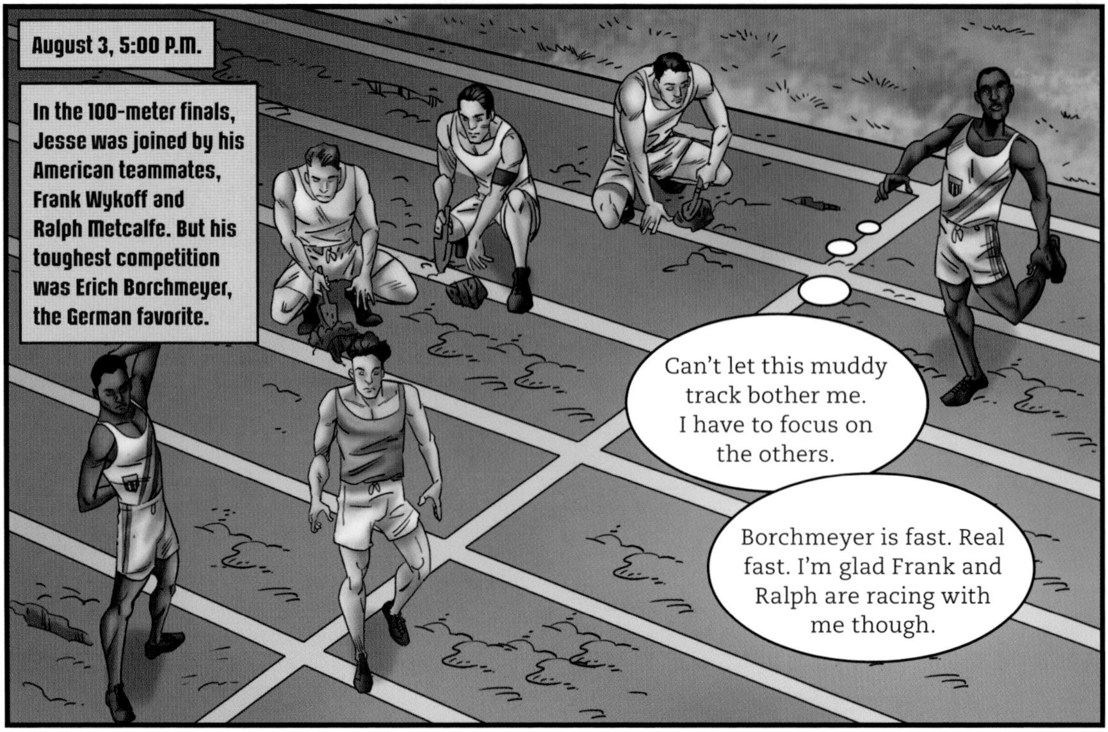
August 3, 5:00 P.M.
In the 100-meter finals, Jesse was joined by his American teammates, Frank Wykoff and Ralph Metcalfe. But his toughest competition was Erich Borchmeyer, the German favorite.
Can't let this muddy track bother me. I have to focus on the others.
Borchmeyer is fast. Real fast. I'm glad Frank and Ralph are racing with me though.

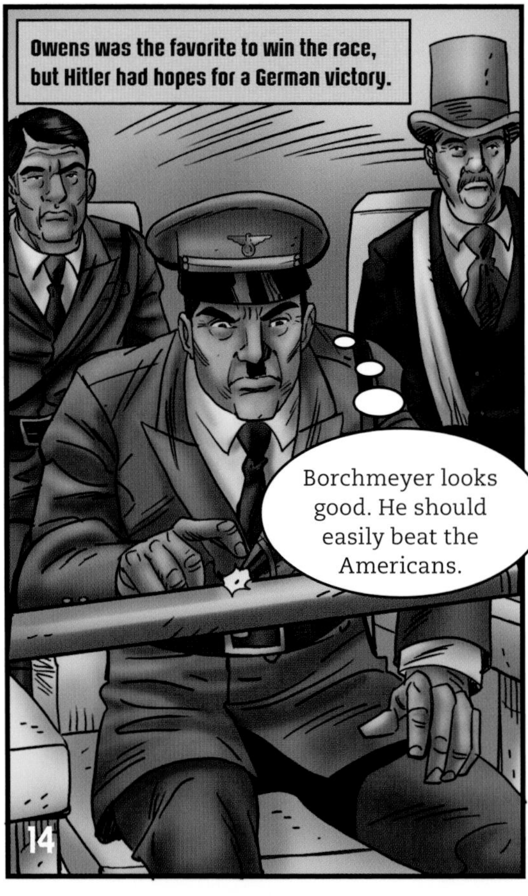
Owens was the favorite to win the race, but Hitler had hopes for a German victory.
Borchmeyer looks good. He should easily beat the Americans.

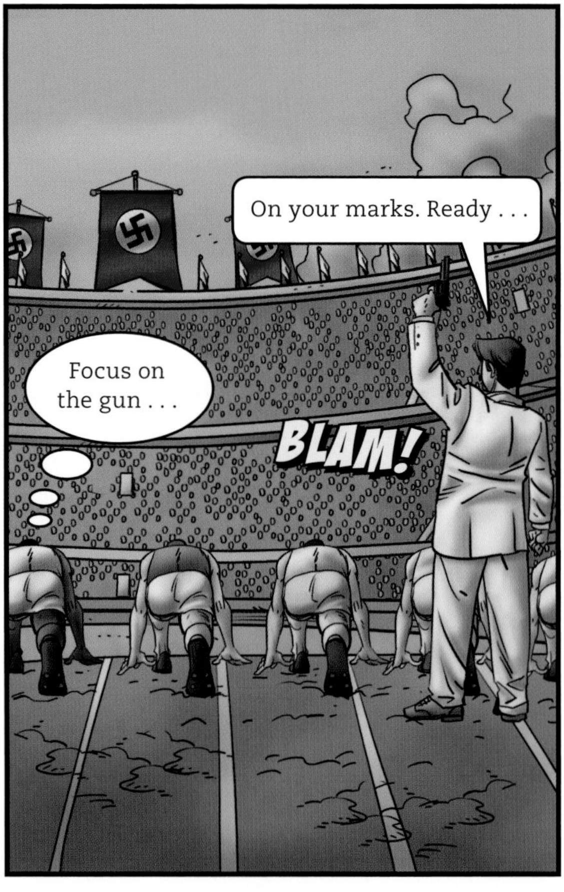
On your marks. Ready . . .
Focus on the gun . . .
BLAM!

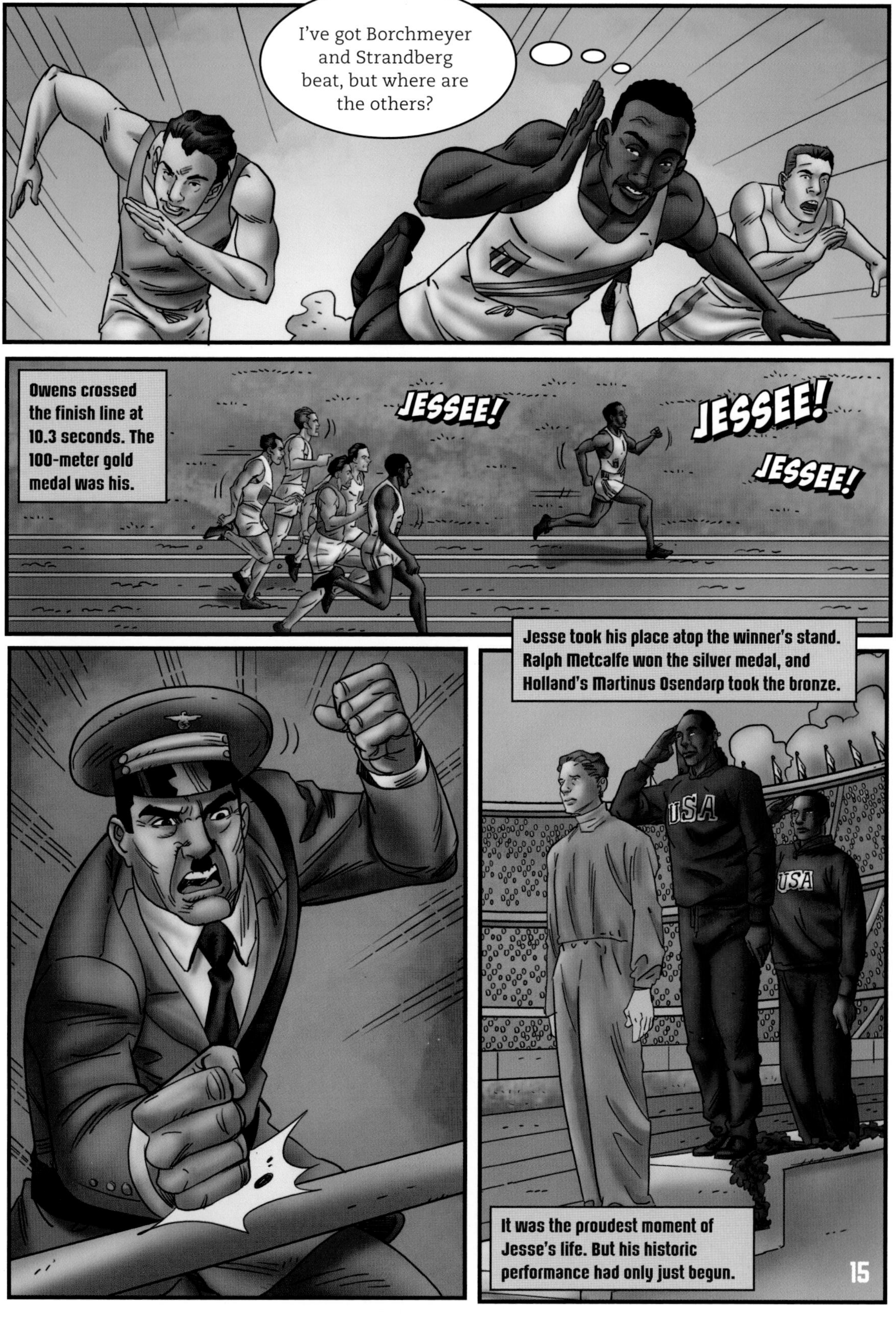
I've got Borchmeyer and Strandberg beat, but where are the others?
Owens crossed the finish line at 10.3 seconds. The 100-meter gold medal was his.
JESSEE!
JESSEE!
JESSEE!
Jesse took his place atop the winner's stand. Ralph Metcalfe won the silver medal, and Holland's Martinus Osendarp took the bronze.
USA
USA
It was the proudest moment of Jesse's life. But his historic performance had only just begun.

BRINGING HOME THE GOLD

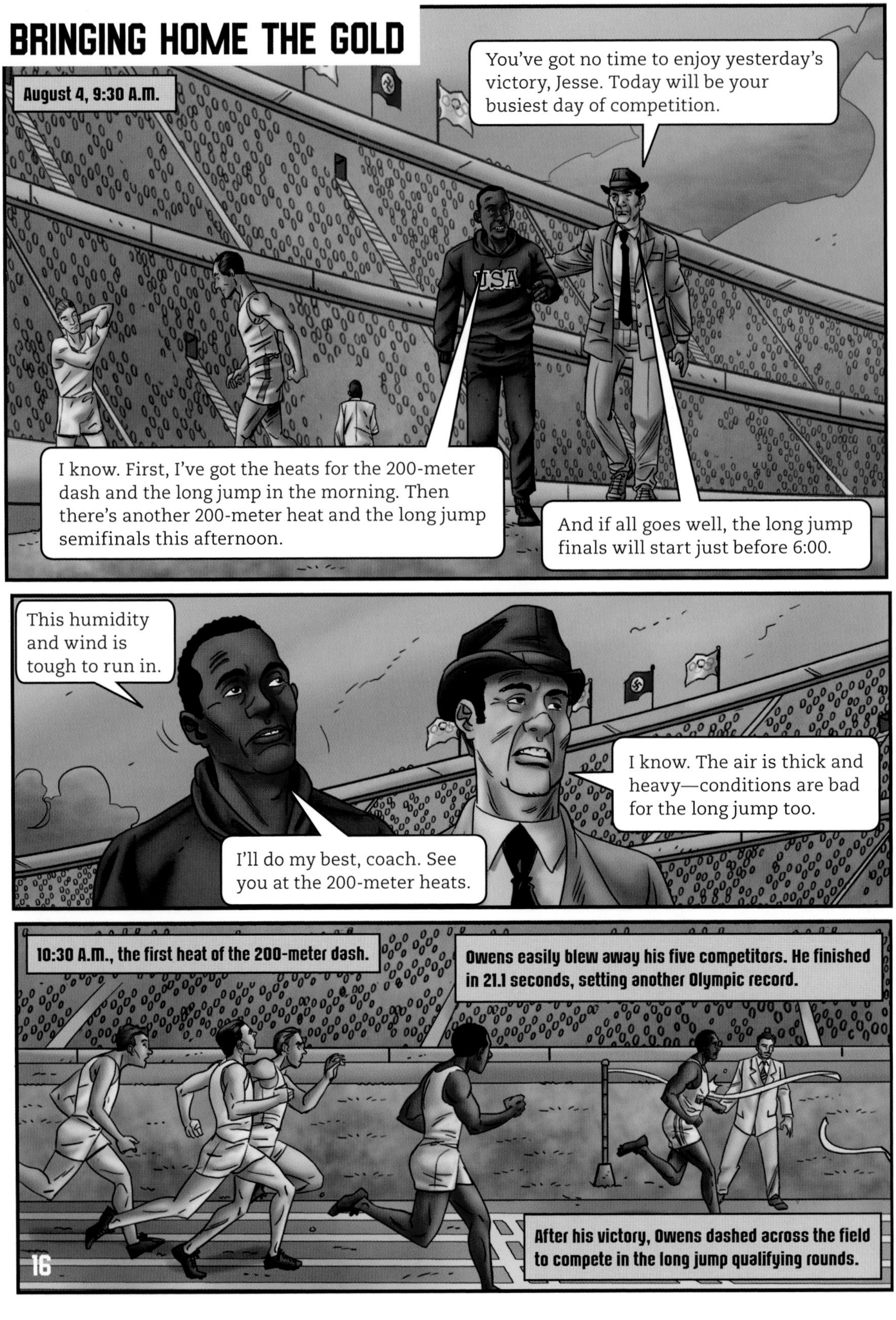
August 4, 9:30 A.M.
You've got no time to enjoy yesterday's victory, Jesse. Today will be your busiest day of competition.
I know. First, I've got the heats for the 200-meter dash and the long jump in the morning. Then there's another 200-meter heat and the long jump semifinals this afternoon.
And if all goes well, the long jump finals will start just before 6:00.
This humidity and wind is tough to run in.
I know. The air is thick and heavy—conditions are bad for the long jump too.
I'll do my best, coach. See you at the 200-meter heats.
10:30 A.M., the first heat of the 200-meter dash.
Owens easily blew away his five competitors. He finished in 21.1 seconds, setting another Olympic record.
After his victory, Owens dashed across the field to compete in the long jump qualifying rounds.

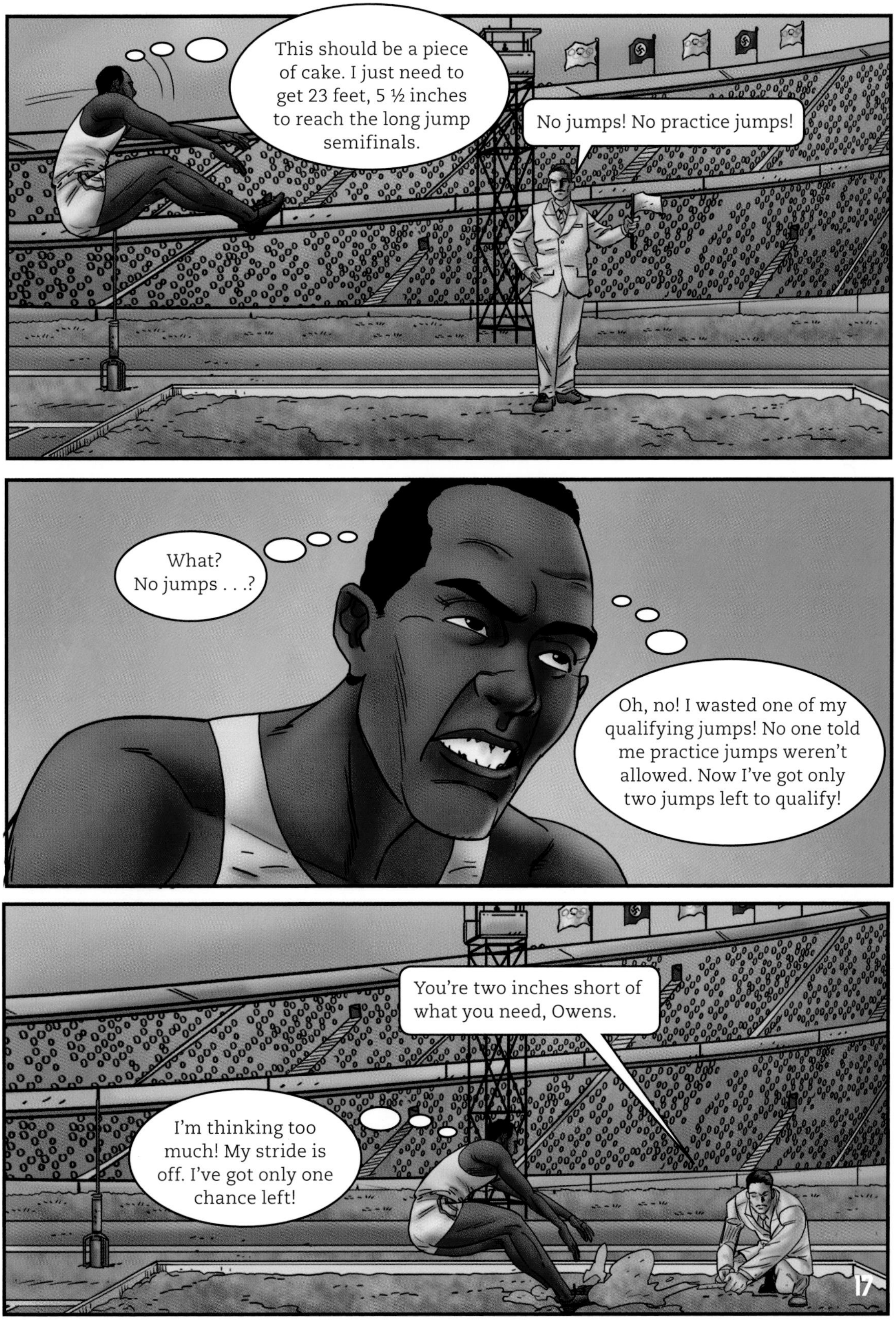
This should be a piece of cake. I just need to get 23 feet, 5 ½ inches to reach the long jump semifinals.
No jumps! No practice jumps!
What? No jumps . . .?
Oh, no! I wasted one of my qualifying jumps! No one told me practice jumps weren't allowed. Now I've got only two jumps left to qualify!
You're two inches short of what you need, Owens.
I'm thinking too much! My stride is off. I've got only one chance left!

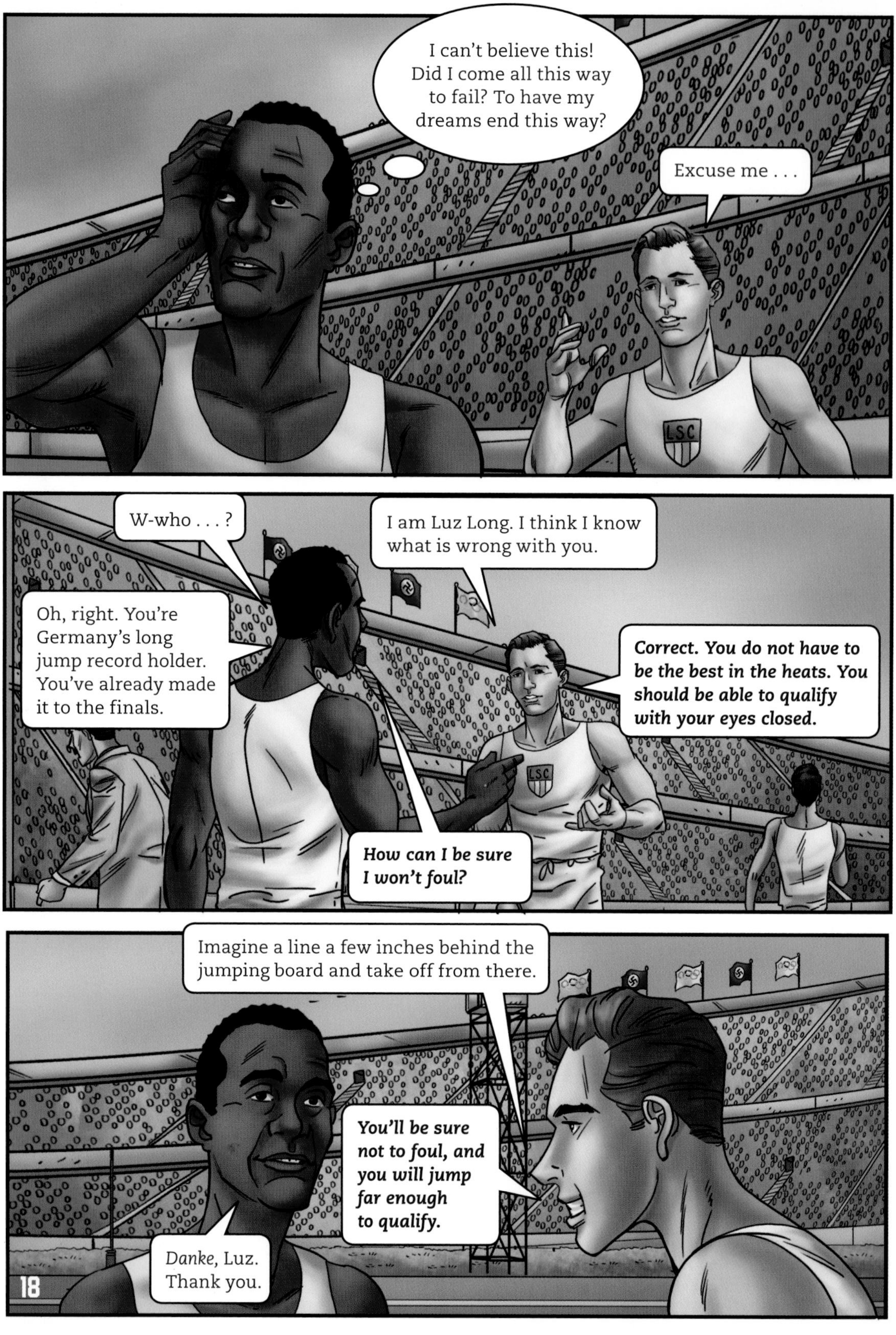
I can't believe this! Did I come all this way to fail? To have my dreams end this way?
Excuse me . . .
W-who . . . ?
I am Luz Long. I think I know what is wrong with you.
Oh, right. You're Germany's long jump record holder. You've already made it to the finals.
Correct. You do not have to be the best in the heats. You should be able to qualify with your eyes closed.
How can I be sure I won't foul?
Imagine a line a few inches behind the jumping board and take off from there.
You'll be sure not to foul, and you will jump far enough to qualify.
Danke, Luz. Thank you.

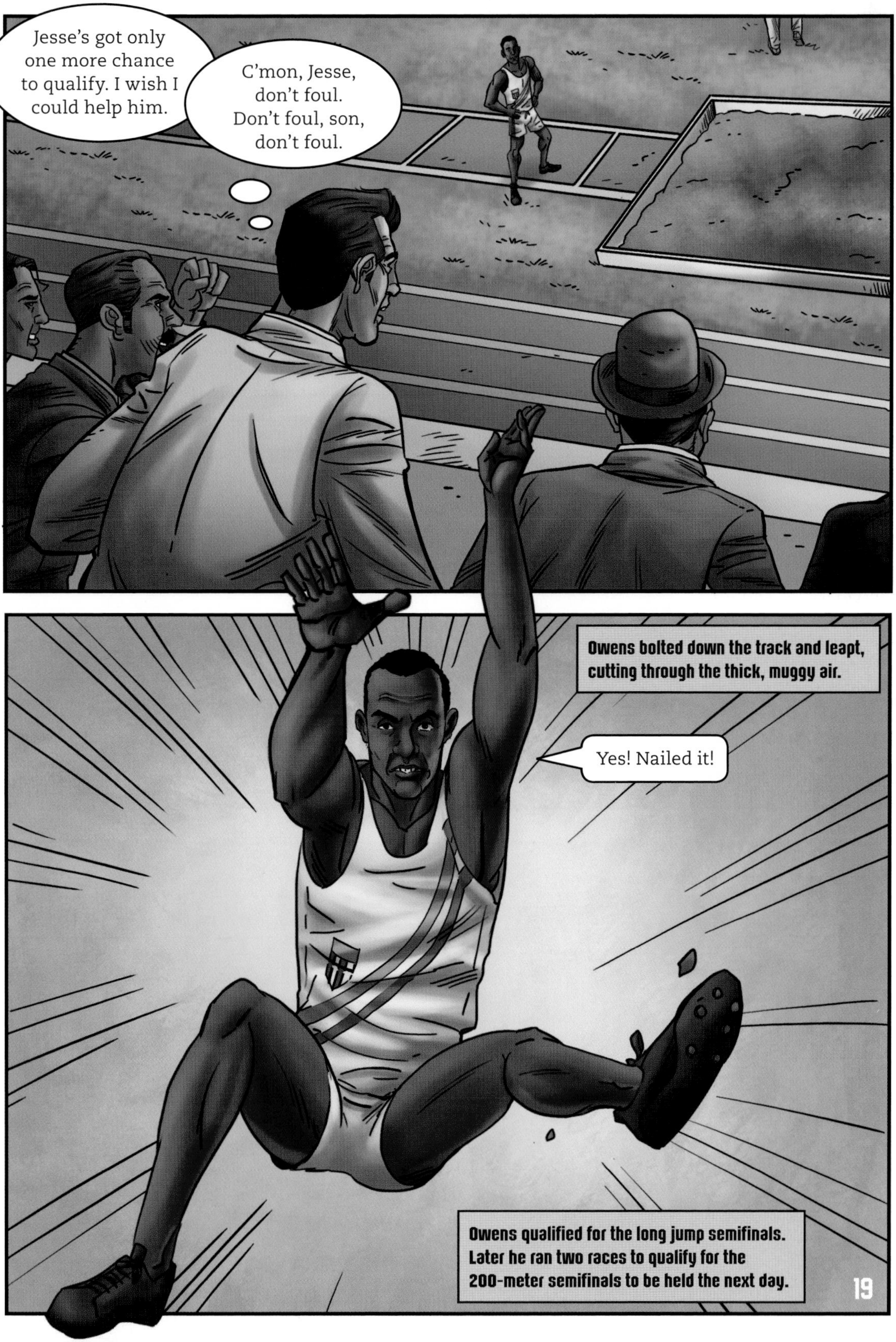
Jesse's got only one more chance to qualify. I wish I could help him.
C'mon, Jesse, don't foul. Don't foul, son, don't foul.
Owens bolted down the track and leapt, cutting through the thick, muggy air.
Yes! Nailed it!
Owens qualified for the long jump semifinals. Later he ran two races to qualify for the 200-meter semifinals to be held the next day.

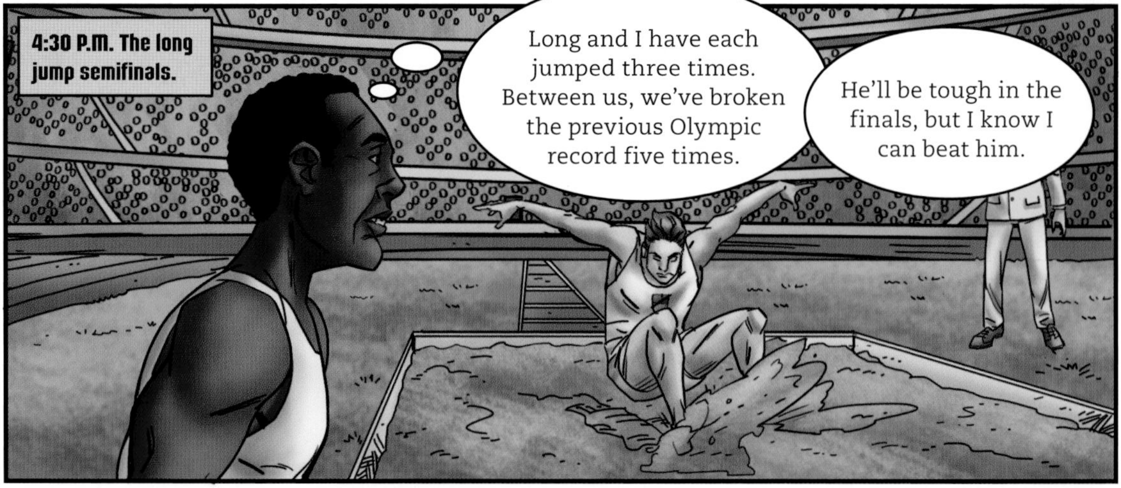
4:30 P.M. The long jump semifinals.
Long and I have each jumped three times. Between us, we've broken the previous Olympic record five times.
He'll be tough in the finals, but I know I can beat him.

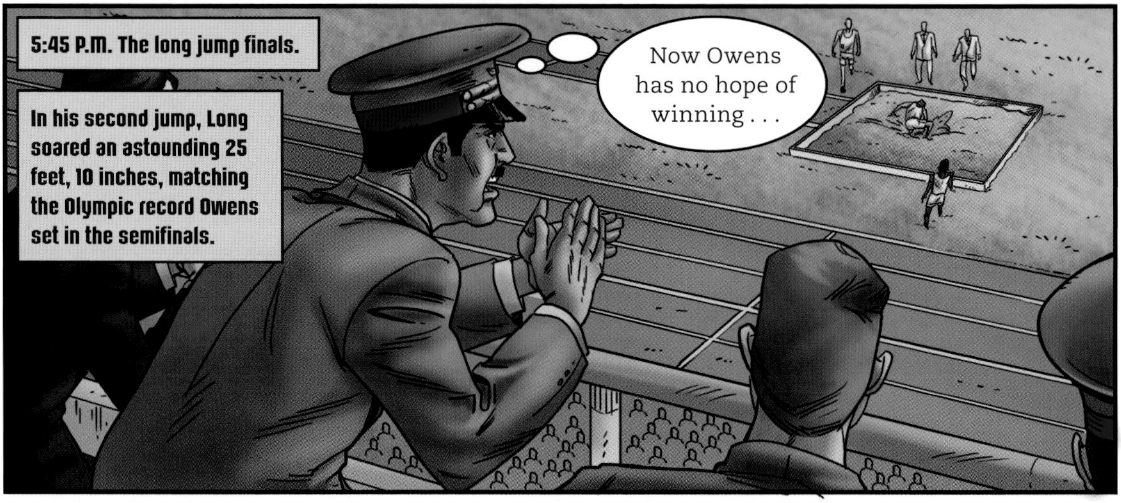
5:45 P.M. The long jump finals.
In his second jump, Long soared an astounding 25 feet, 10 inches, matching the Olympic record Owens set in the semifinals.
Now Owens has no hope of winning . . .

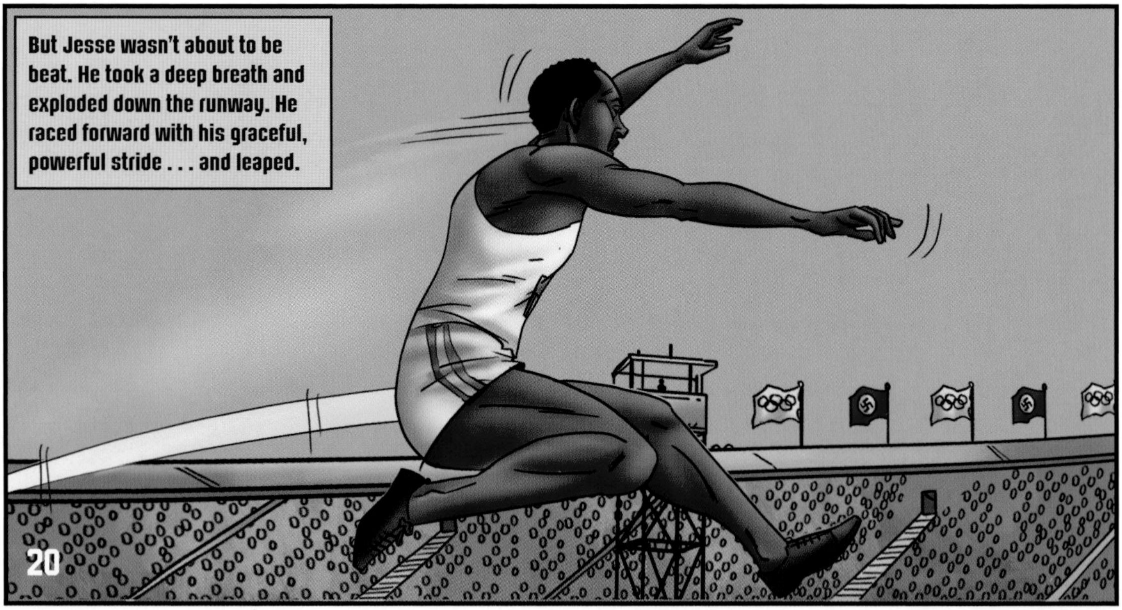
But Jesse wasn't about to be beat. He took a deep breath and exploded down the runway. He raced forward with his graceful, powerful stride . . . and leaped.

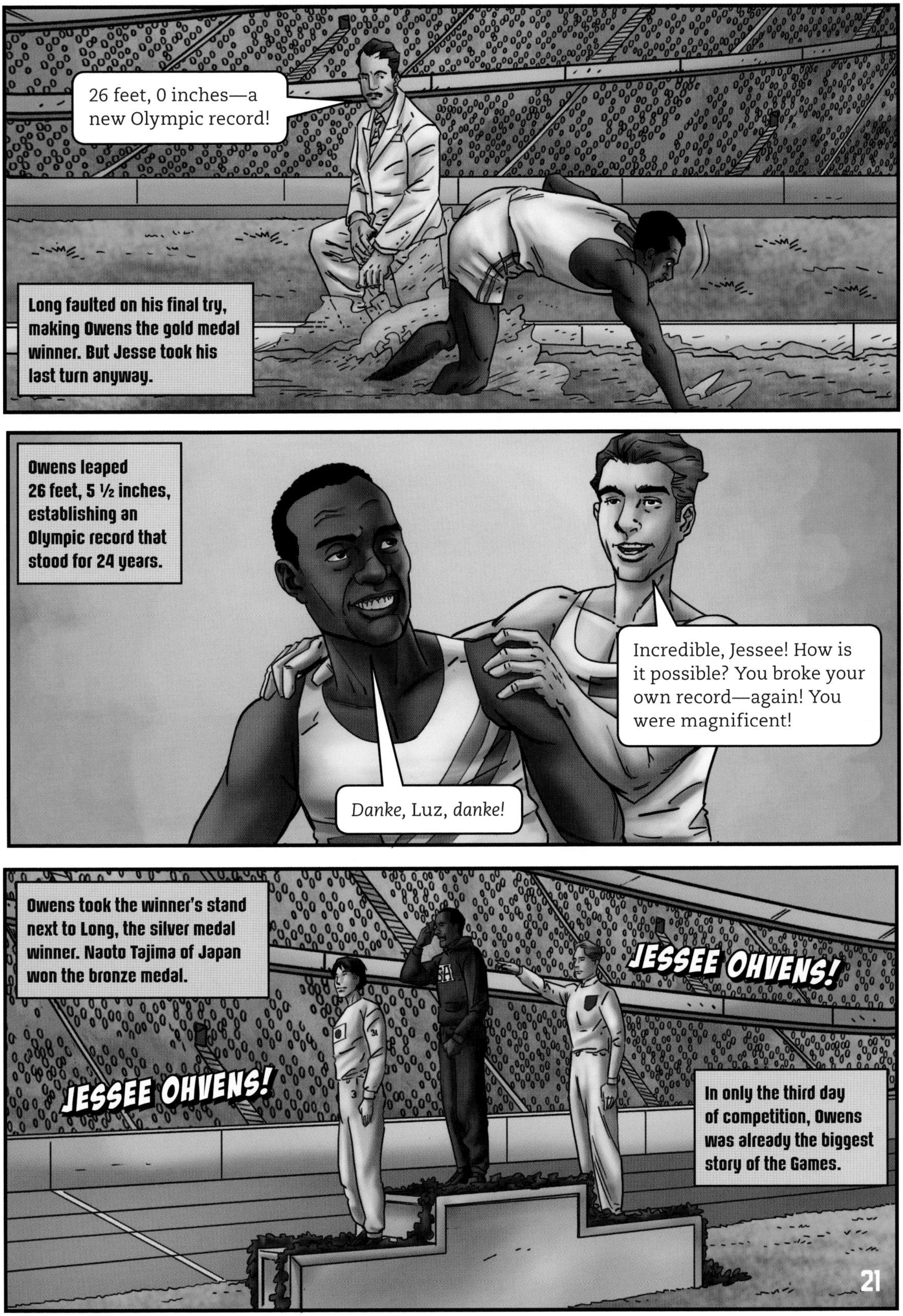

26 feet, 0 inches—a new Olympic record!
Long faulted on his final try, making Owens the gold medal winner. But Jesse took his last turn anyway.
Owens leaped 26 feet, 5 ½ inches, establishing an Olympic record that stood for 24 years.
Incredible, Jessee! How is it possible? You broke your own record—again! You were magnificent!
Danke, Luz, *danke*!
Owens took the winner's stand next to Long, the silver medal winner. Naoto Tajima of Japan won the bronze medal.
JESSEE OHVENS!
JESSEE OHVENS!
In only the third day of competition, Owens was already the biggest story of the Games.

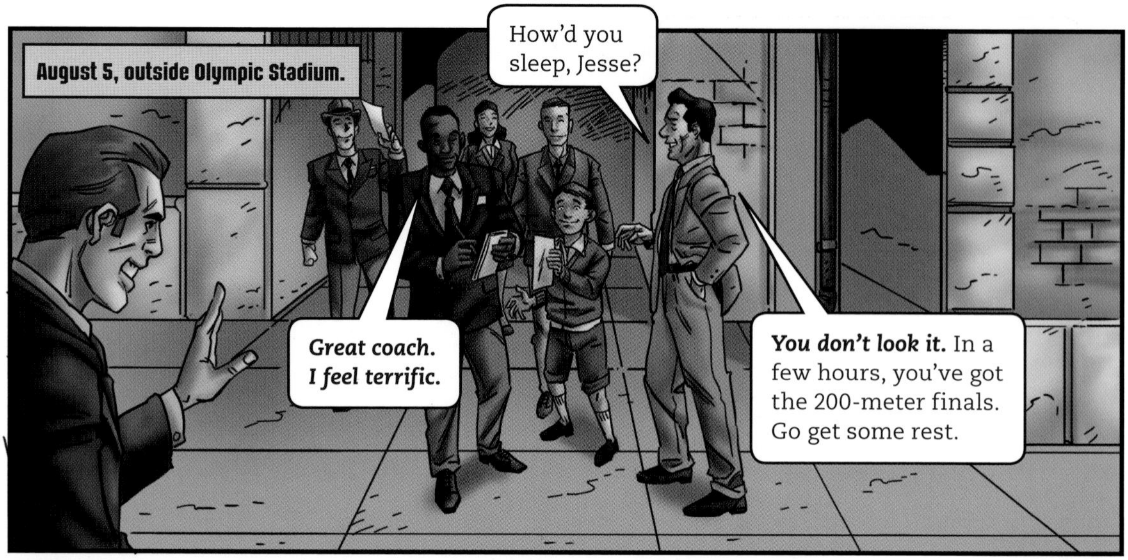
August 5, outside Olympic Stadium.
How'd you sleep, Jesse?
Great coach. I feel terrific.
You don't look it. In a few hours, you've got the 200-meter finals. Go get some rest.

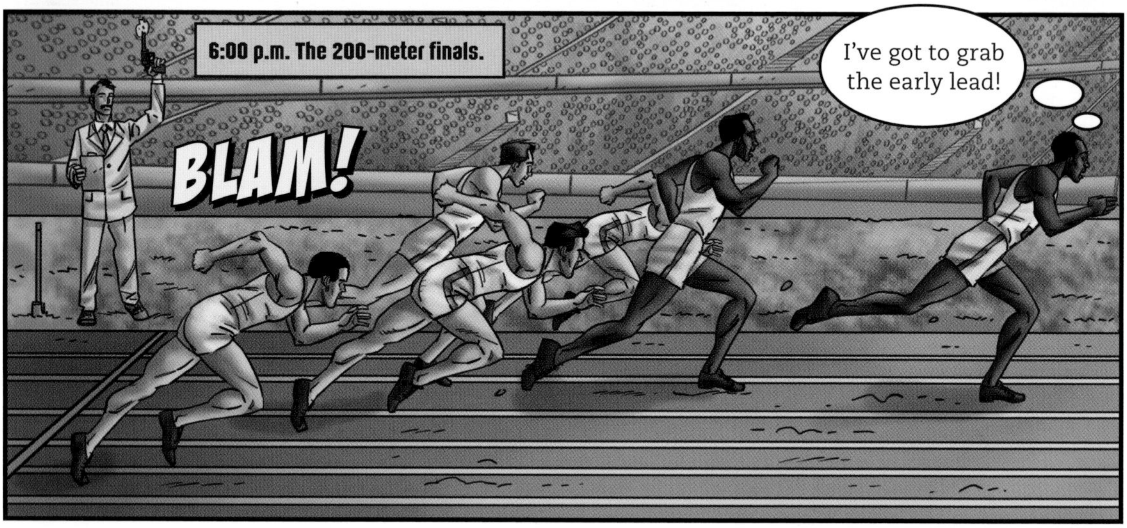
6:00 p.m. The 200-meter finals.
BLAM!
I've got to grab the early lead!

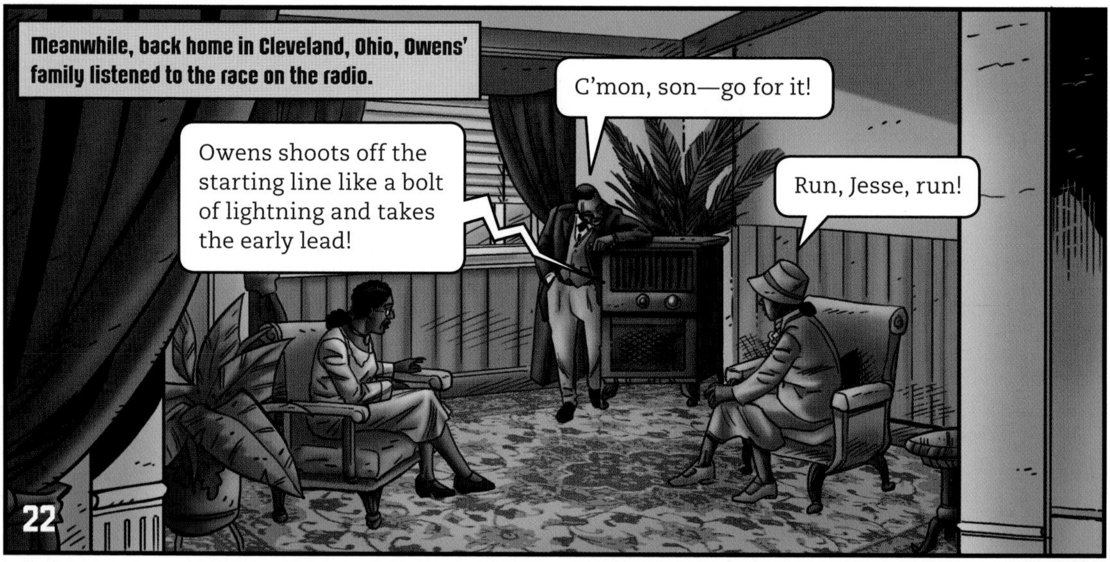
Meanwhile, back home in Cleveland, Ohio, Owens' family listened to the race on the radio.
Owens shoots off the starting line like a bolt of lightning and takes the early lead!
C'mon, son—go for it!
Run, Jesse, run!

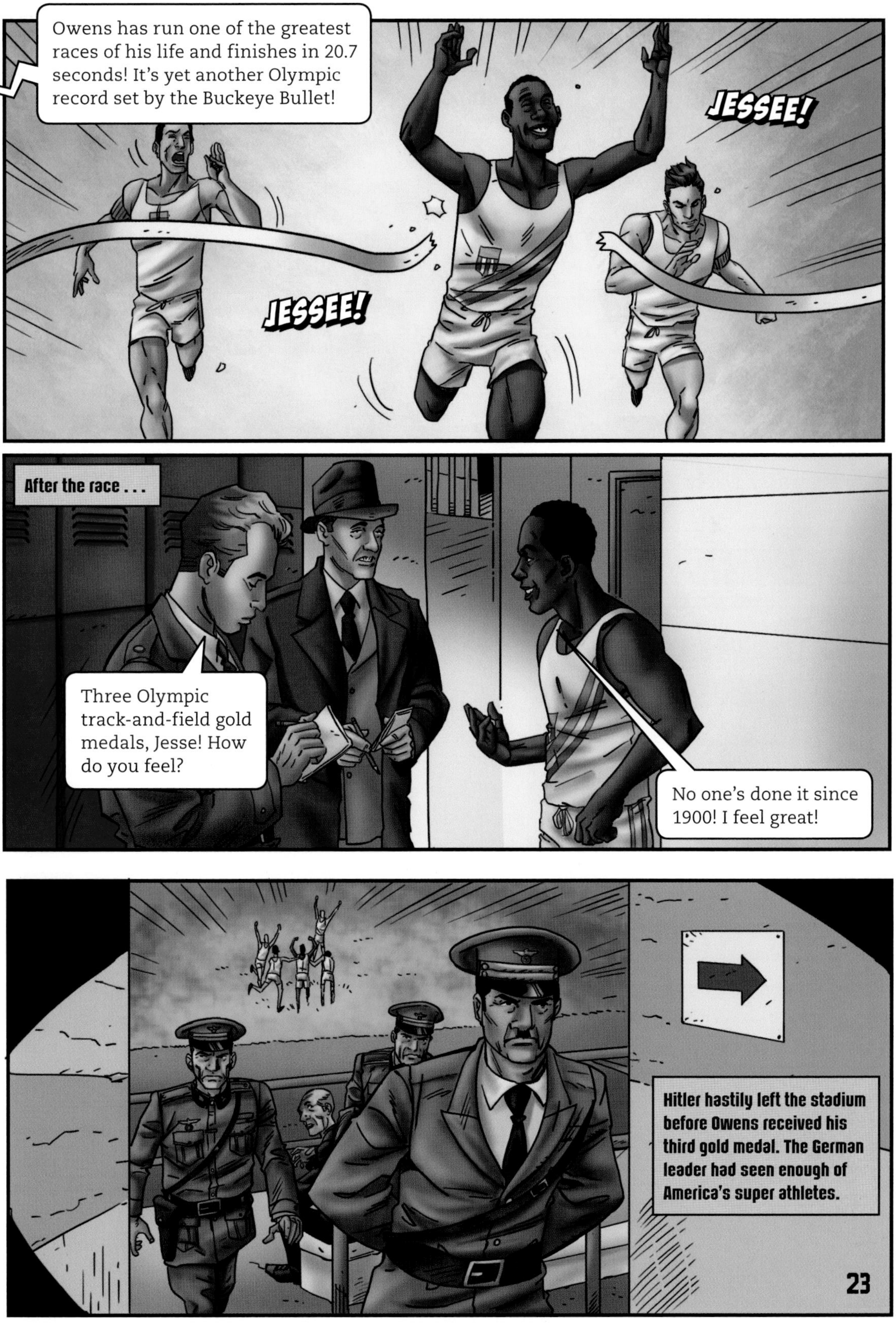
Owens has run one of the greatest races of his life and finishes in 20.7 seconds! It's yet another Olympic record set by the Buckeye Bullet!
JESSEE!
JESSEE!
After the race . . .
Three Olympic track-and-field gold medals, Jesse! How do you feel?
No one's done it since 1900! I feel great!
Hitler hastily left the stadium before Owens received his third gold medal. The German leader had seen enough of America's super athletes.

THE FINAL RUN

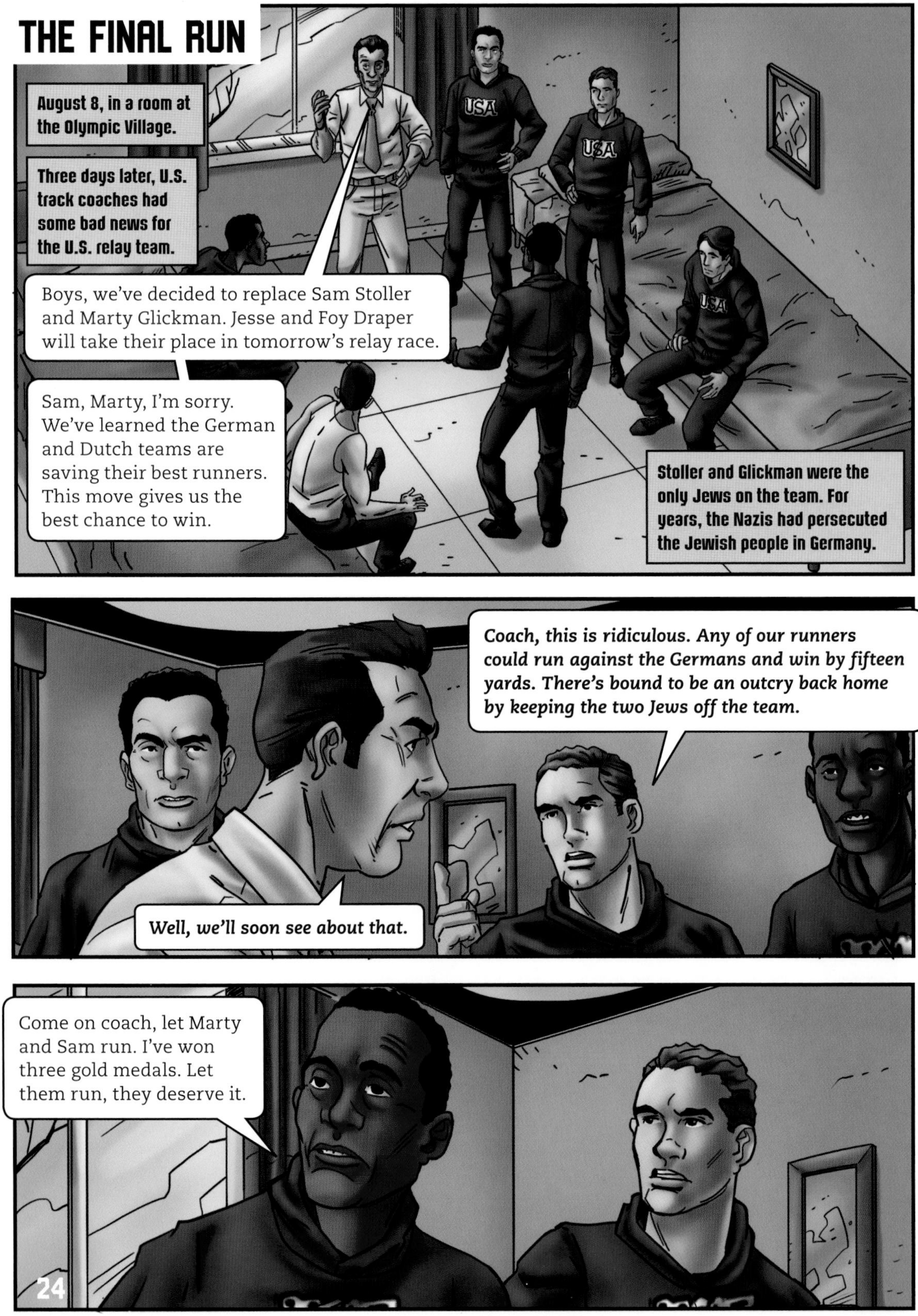
August 8, in a room at the Olympic Village.
Three days later, U.S. track coaches had some bad news for the U.S. relay team.
Boys, we've decided to replace Sam Stoller and Marty Glickman. Jesse and Foy Draper will take their place in tomorrow's relay race.
Sam, Marty, I'm sorry. We've learned the German and Dutch teams are saving their best runners. This move gives us the best chance to win.
Stoller and Glickman were the only Jews on the team. For years, the Nazis had persecuted the Jewish people in Germany.
Coach, this is ridiculous. Any of our runners could run against the Germans and win by fifteen yards. There's bound to be an outcry back home by keeping the two Jews off the team.
Well, we'll soon see about that.
Come on coach, let Marty and Sam run. I've won three gold medals. Let them run, they deserve it.

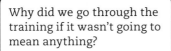

Why did we go through the training if it wasn't going to mean anything?

With all due respect, Foy finished last—Marty and I beat him.

Sam, **Foy has more experience. That's our decision.** End of discussion.

Did American Olympic officials want to save Hitler the embarrassment of losing the race to Jews? It's impossible to know for certain.

However, the decision had been made. The coaches believed that Owens and Draper gave the American team a better chance to win the relay race.

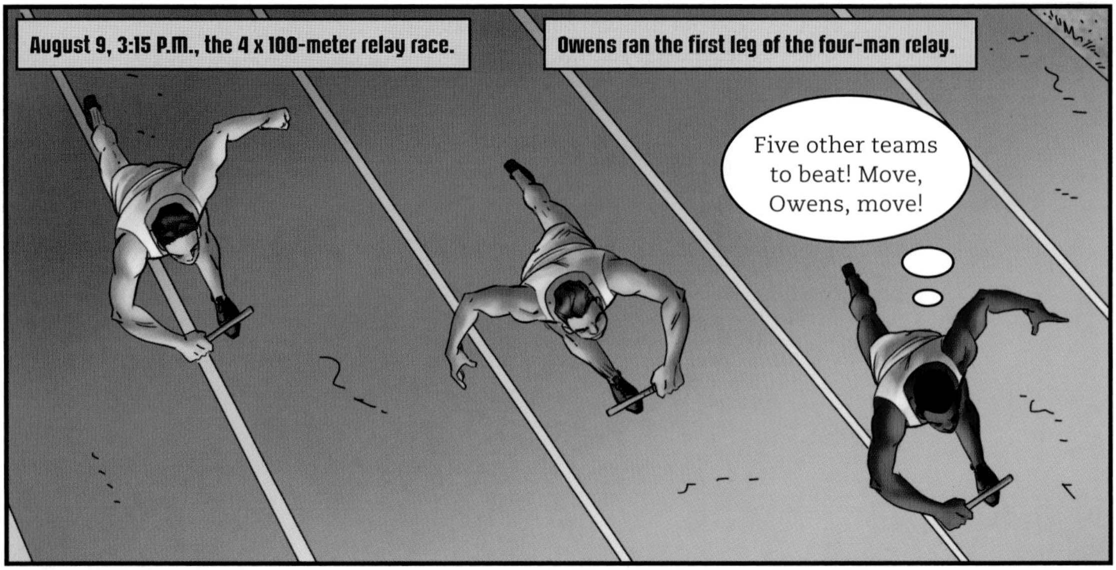
August 9, 3:15 P.M., the 4 x 100-meter relay race.
Owens ran the first leg of the four-man relay.
Five other teams to beat! Move, Owens, move!

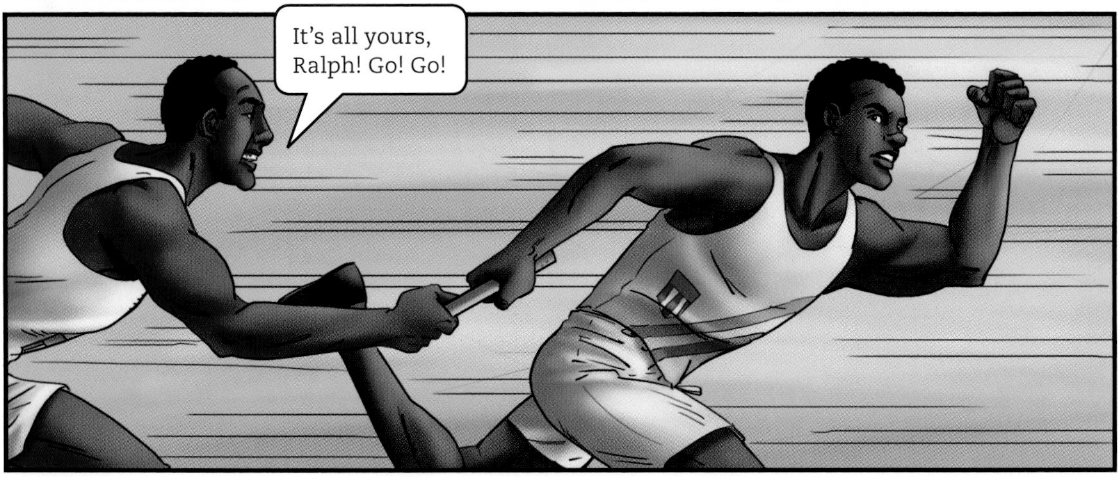
It's all yours, Ralph! Go! Go!

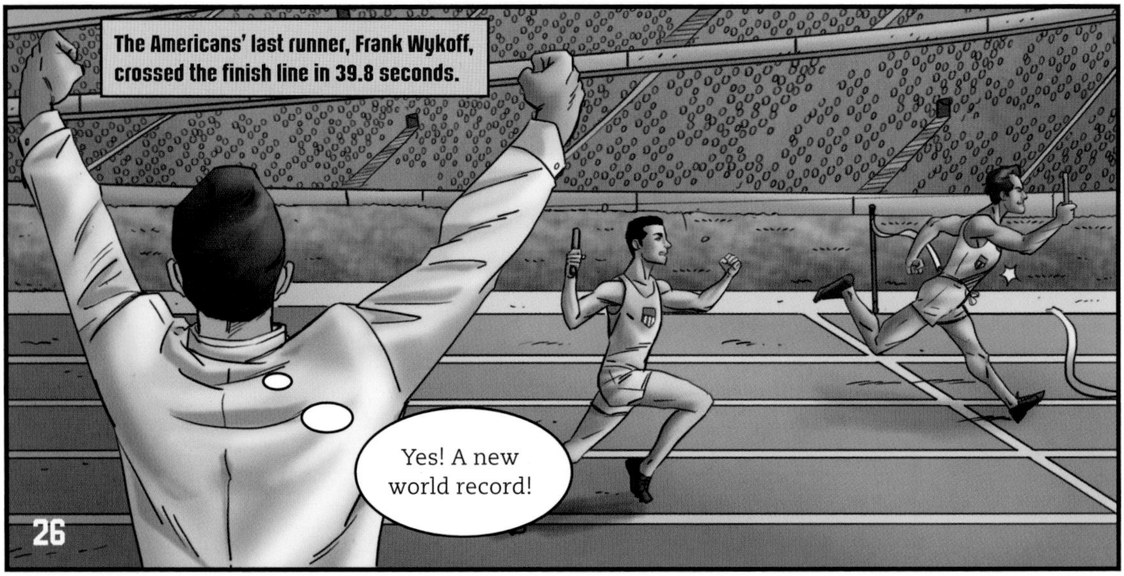
The Americans' last runner, Frank Wykoff, crossed the finish line in 39.8 seconds.
Yes! A new world record!

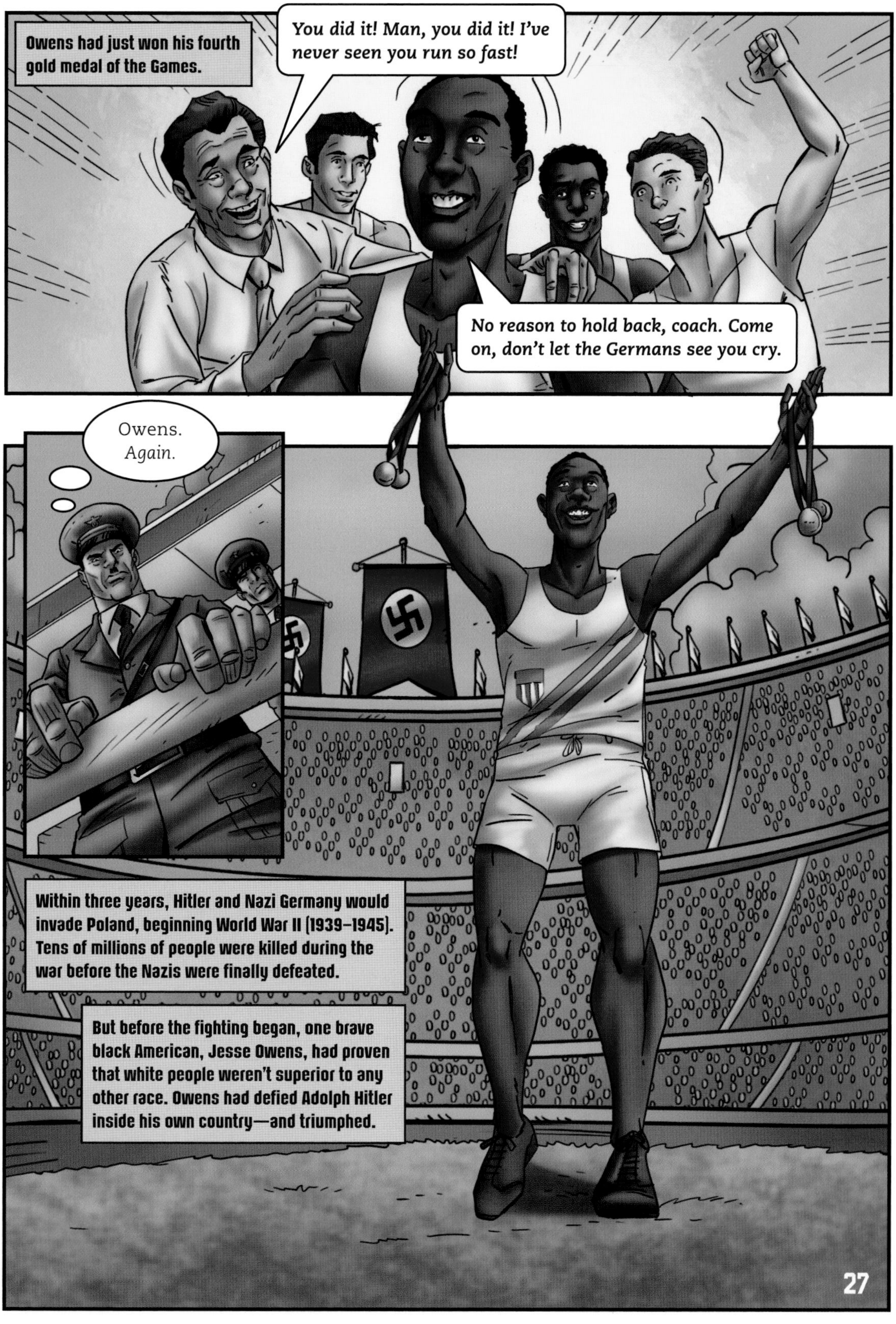
Owens had just won his fourth gold medal of the Games.
You did it! Man, you did it! I've never seen you run so fast!
No reason to hold back, coach. Come on, don't let the Germans see you cry.
Owens. Again.
Within three years, Hitler and Nazi Germany would invade Poland, beginning World War II (1939–1945). Tens of millions of people were killed during the war before the Nazis were finally defeated.
But before the fighting began, one brave black American, Jesse Owens, had proven that white people weren't superior to any other race. Owens had defied Adolph Hitler inside his own country—and triumphed.

MEETING LIFE'S CHALLENGES

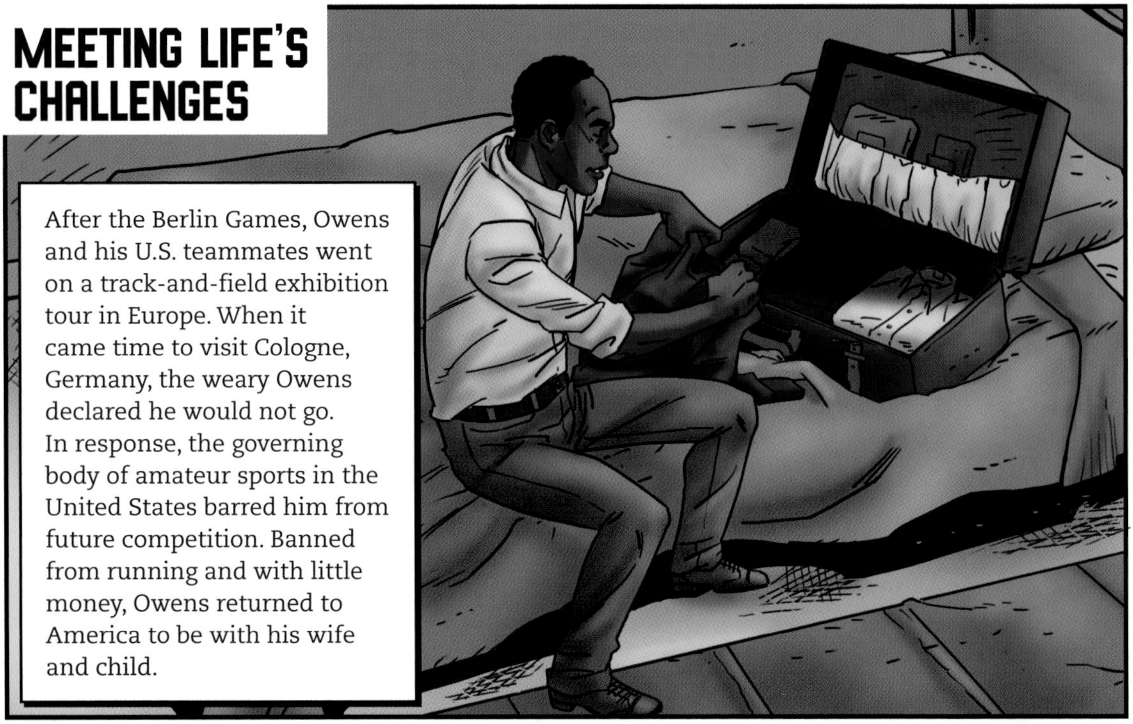
After the Berlin Games, Owens and his U.S. teammates went on a track-and-field exhibition tour in Europe. When it came time to visit Cologne, Germany, the weary Owens declared he would not go. In response, the governing body of amateur sports in the United States barred him from future competition. Banned from running and with little money, Owens returned to America to be with his wife and child.

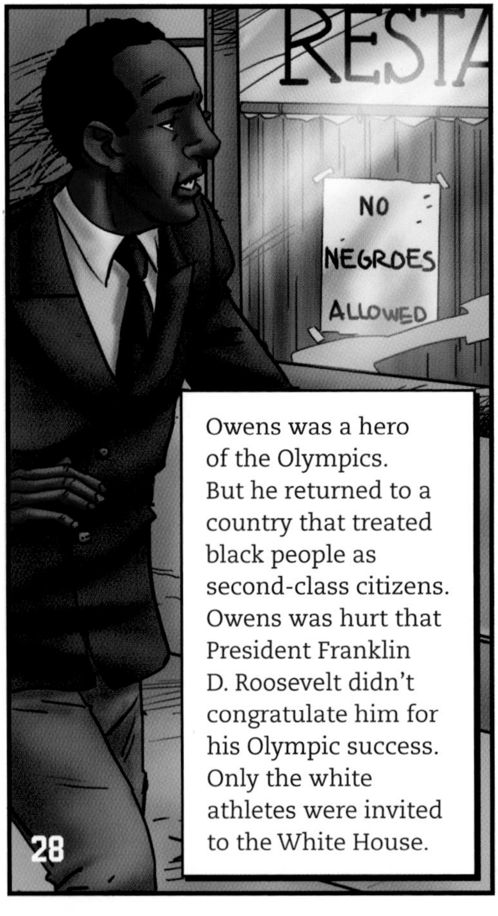
RESTA
NO
NEGROES
ALLOWED
Owens was a hero of the Olympics. But he returned to a country that treated black people as second-class citizens. Owens was hurt that President Franklin D. Roosevelt didn't congratulate him for his Olympic success. Only the white athletes were invited to the White House.

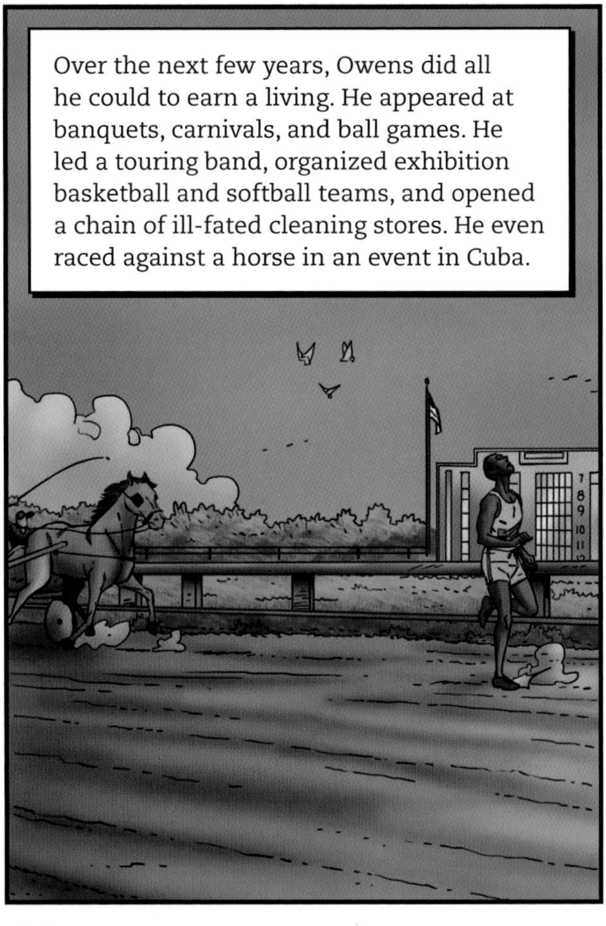
Over the next few years, Owens did all he could to earn a living. He appeared at banquets, carnivals, and ball games. He led a touring band, organized exhibition basketball and softball teams, and opened a chain of ill-fated cleaning stores. He even raced against a horse in an event in Cuba.

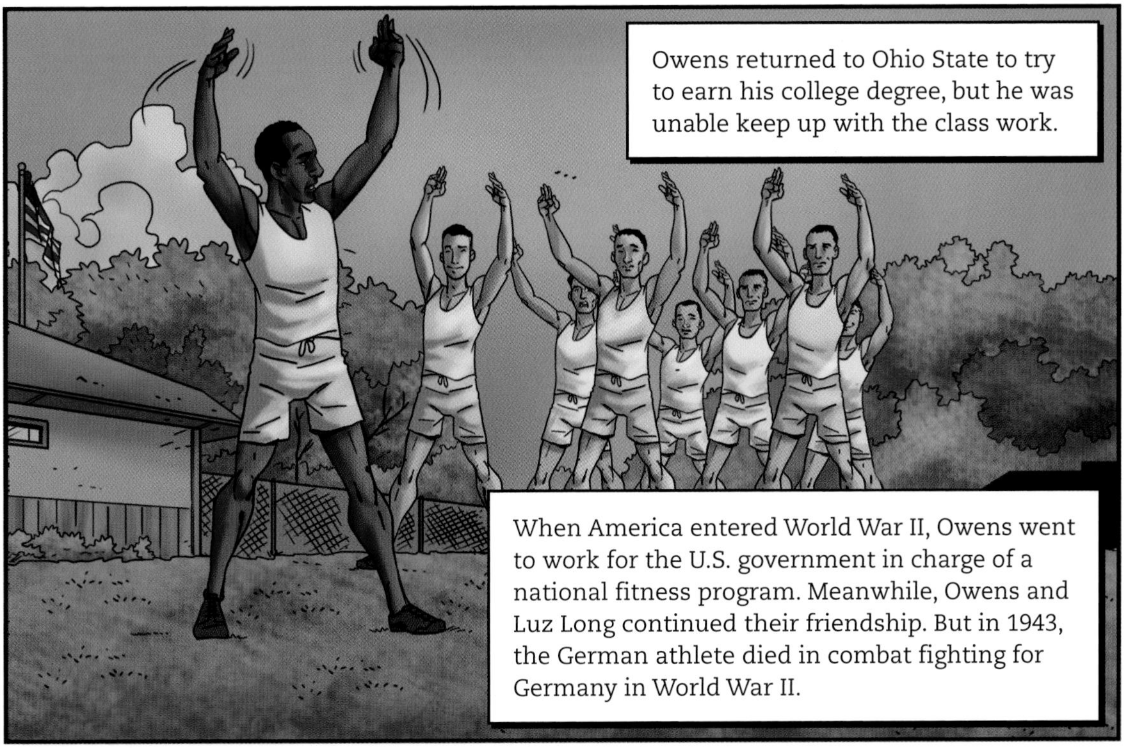
Owens returned to Ohio State to try to earn his college degree, but he was unable keep up with the class work.
When America entered World War II, Owens went to work for the U.S. government in charge of a national fitness program. Meanwhile, Owens and Luz Long continued their friendship. But in 1943, the German athlete died in combat fighting for Germany in World War II.

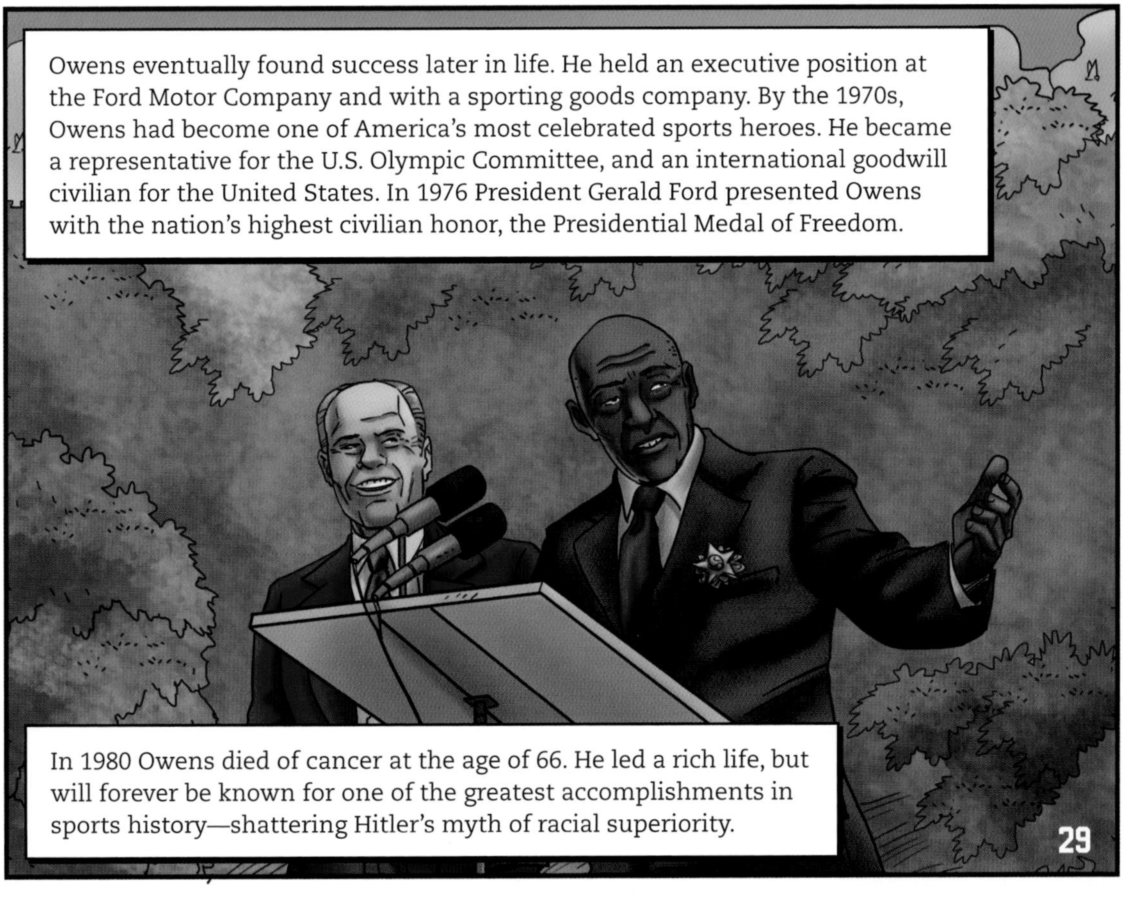
Owens eventually found success later in life. He held an executive position at the Ford Motor Company and with a sporting goods company. By the 1970s, Owens had become one of America's most celebrated sports heroes. He became a representative for the U.S. Olympic Committee, and an international goodwill civilian for the United States. In 1976 President Gerald Ford presented Owens with the nation's highest civilian honor, the Presidential Medal of Freedom.
In 1980 Owens died of cancer at the age of 66. He led a rich life, but will forever be known for one of the greatest accomplishments in sports history—shattering Hitler's myth of racial superiority.

GLOSSARY

boycott (BOY-kot)—to refuse to take part in something as a way of making a protest

chancellor (CHAN-suh-lur)—the title for the leader of a country

civilian (si-VIL-yuhn)—someone who is not a member of the armed forces

discrimination (dis-kri-muh-NAY-shun)—the unfair treatment of people because of their race, country of birth, religious beliefs, or gender

heat (HEET)—an early round of a competition to determine who will advance to the finals

outcry (OUT-krye)—loud protests or complaints from many people

shun (SHUHN)—to avoid or ignore someone or something on purpose

supremacy (soo-PREM-uh-see)—the state of being superior, or having supreme power or authority

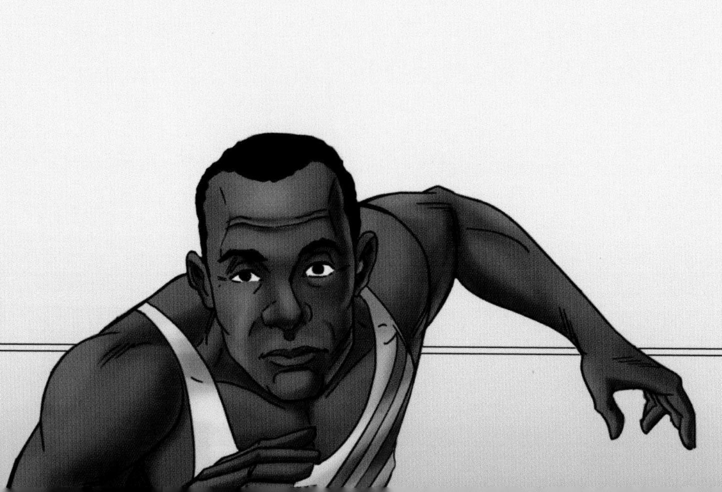

READ MORE

Buckley, James Jr. *Who Was Jesse Owens?* New York: Grosset & Dunlap, 2015.

Burgan, Michael. *Olympic Gold 1936: How the Image of Jesse Owens Crushed Hitler's Evil Myth.* North Mankato, MN: Compass Point Books, 2017.

Stanmyre, Jackie F. *Jesse Owens: Facing Down Hitler.* New York: Cavendish Square Publishing, 2016.

CRITICAL THINKING QUESTIONS

- Many Americans favored a boycott of the 1936 Olympics to protest Hitler and the Nazis. Do you think the U.S. team should have stayed home? Why?

- Put yourself in Hitler's place. How would you feel about the Americans' victories? Why do you think it was painful to him that black athletes won so many events?

- Owens ran to win. Do you think he saw himself as a "weapon" against Nazism? Why or why not?

INTERNET SITES

Use Facthound to find Internet sites related
to this book.

Visit *www.facthound.com*

Just type in 9781543528657 and go.

Super-cool stuff! Check out projects, games and lots more at www.capstonekids.com

INDEX

boycott, 6, 7

Hitler, Adolph, 4, 5, 7, 9, 11, 14, 20, 23,
    25, 27, 29

Jews, 4, 6, 7, 24, 25

Long, Luz, 18, 20, 21, 29

Nazis, 4, 6, 7, 9, 13, 24, 27

Olympic events
    100-meter dash, 6, 10–15
    200-meter dash, 6, 16, 19, 22
    long jump, 6, 16, 17–21
    relay race, 24–27
Olympic Village, 8, 13, 24
Owens, Jesse
    death, 29

family, 5, 22, 28
life after Olympics, 28–29
medals, 7, 9, 15, 21, 24, 27
nickname, 23
Ohio State University, 5, 29
Presidential Medal of Freedom, 29
records, 5, 6, 11, 12, 13, 16, 20,
    21, 23, 26
U.S. Olympic Committee, 29

racism, 4, 5, 7, 9, 27, 28, 29

teammates, 8, 10, 13, 14, 15,
    24–25, 26

U.S. presidents, 28, 29

World War II, 27, 29